Thread Painting

Simple Techniques to Add Texture and Dimension

©2007 Leni Levenson Wiener

Published by

An Imprint of F+W Publications

700 East State Street • Iola, WI 54990-0001
715-445-2214 • 888-457-2873
www.krausebooks.com

Our toll-free number to place an order or obtain a free catalog is (800) 258-0929.

The following registered trademark terms and companies appear in this publication:

Adobe®, Baby Lock®, American & Efird™, Atlas Gloves, Bernina®, Brother®, Bubble Jet Set 2000™, Bubble Jet Set™ Rinse, C. Jenkins Company, Carol Doak, Coats and Clark Dual Duty™ Plus, Clover Needlecraft, ColorPlus®, Color Textiles, Electric Quilt™, Elna™, Expo International, EZ Quilting™ by Wrights™, Fairfield Processing Corp., Fiskars®, Free Spirit Fabrics, Hobbs Bonded Fibers, Husqvarna® Viking®, iPod™, Janome™, June Tailor®, Kenmore™, Michael Miller Fabrics, Nitrile Touch™ Quilter's Gloves, Olfa™, Pellon™, Pfaff™, Photoshop®, Elements, Poly-fil™, Printed Treasures™, Prym™ Consumer USA, RJR Fabrics™, Robison-Anton™ Threads, Rowenta™, Roxanne Products, Schmetz™ Needles, Singer®, Sulky® of America, Superior Threads, Tacony™, The Warm™ Company, White Sewing Machine™, Wonderfil

Library of Congress Control Number: 2006935439

ISBN-13: 978-0-89689-435-8

ISBN-10: 0-89689-435-5

Designed by Emily Adler

Edited by Linda Turner Griepentrog

Printed in China

Acknowledgments

I would like to thank the following people for their assistance in the preparation of this book:

- Krause Acquisitions Editor Candy Wiza, for her constant support and believing in me in the first place; and for everyone at Krause who answered my questions and held my hand along the way.
- Linda Griepentrog, for editing the manuscript.
- Emily Adler, for her beautiful design work.
- Bob Best, for his wonderful photography.
- My "test" elves, whose feedback was so important: Connie Benson, Denise Bradley, Elaine Conroy, Kathi Jahnke and Peggy Young.
- Lori Dvir-Djerassi from Color Textiles, for technical information, as well as the ColorPlus fabrics used for all the samples in the book.
- Tammie Bowser and Stephanie Kimura, for "showing me the ropes."
- Special thanks to the companies who generously provided materials to complete the projects and samples in the book – they are noted in the Resource section of the book.
- My friends who put up with my endless discussions about the book for many months.
- Zachary Ehrenreich, for the use of his inspiring artwork.
- And finally, my family — husband Fred, and sons Jared and Jordan — who kept me laughing and supported my efforts all the way through; and my parents, Helene and Ed Levenson, for their constant support and encouragement.

Introduction

Think of the sewing machine needle as a pencil or paintbrush. That is the simple start of thread painting — guiding the thread the way a talented artist guides a paintbrush to literally "paint" with thread.

Thread painting is an adaptation of free-motion quilting, which you may already know how to do. When free-motion quilting, the feed dogs are dropped so the machine stitches in place, and you guide the needle the same way an artist guides a paintbrush.

Every quilt show has at least one art piece seemingly done all in stitches. Most often, the artwork started with a fabric painting overlaid with stitches. The painting forms a base with subtle color variations, and helps determine where the stitches will go.

There are books and Web sites that promise an easy way to thread paint; they all invariably start with a design tracing on the fabric. Besides being tedious, tracing is not an ideal way to transfer a design to fabric for thread painting. It is difficult to transfer subtleties where colors blend, and the resulting picture needs to be filled in completely, like a coloring book with black lines on a white page.

Thread painting itself is not hard. The hard part is getting the right image onto the fabric, without losing its subtle color changes and small details. So what about those of us who are not talented artists? That is where this book starts. It is as easy as painting by numbers or coloring in a coloring book. The difference is, you will be using thread and a sewing machine, and you do not need to paint, draw or trace.

The recent introduction of an innovative product — inkjet-printable fabric — makes this technique possible. This special fabric is backed with paper and feeds through a regular inkjet computer printer. When the paper backing is peeled away, the result is a soft printed fabric that can be washed and ironed. It is a wonderful way to transfer photos for memory quilts or to make quilt labels, but it is the best and easiest way to lay a foundation for thread painting. As simple as printing a page, the artwork is "painted" onto fabric, with all the subtle color shading and all the details.

Once the image is printed, all that remains is to "color it in" with thread. Color placement is obvious. Unlike a traced design, not all of the areas need to be completely filled with thread. Some areas can be left with only the printing; others can be lightly stitched so that the printed color shows through. The result is thread painting that is quick, easy and effective, and every bit as amazing as those that started with a painting!

In this book you will learn how to find images that will be appropriate for thread paintings and how to print them on fabric (or where to purchase them already printed). You will also learn what threads to use, how to blend and shade colors, and how to use these "works of art" in quilts, clothing, pillows and accessories.

This is the pillow that inspired me to write this book, although I had no way of knowing it at the time.

I loved the fabric — the rich colors and swirling leaves appealed to me. I started with a piece of fabric and added complementary borders. It needed more, so I cut leaves from leftover fabric and fused them to the border. I used invisible thread to encase the raw edges with a small zigzag stitch. It was still missing something.

I decided to fill in a few of the center leaves with thread to add texture and dimension and create a focal point. Using whatever threads I had on hand, I matched some of the print colors, but sometimes I chose a lighter or darker color for shading. I used a similar color if I did not have an exact match. That added more interest and life to the pillow.

I have used this pillow in my classes for years as an example of how to do machine appliqué, but students are always more interested in the "embroidery" techniques.

I have used inkjet-printable wash-away and tear-away stabilizers for machine quilting for many years. I print the quilt motif onto one of the stabilizers, pin it to the quilt, stitch through it, and then remove it. I can totally avoid marking the quilt top.

While looking for interesting motifs for quilting, I often came across pen-and-ink drawings I thought would look wonderful in thread. It did not take long to decide that tracing them was not the way I wanted to spend my time. The same stabilizers that worked well for me with quilting were the answer. These curtains were the first experiment I did with this technique. I was having a great time doing all sorts of thread sketches!

Shortly after I started thread sketching, I discovered inkjet-printable fabric. I taught memory quilt classes using heat-set photo transfers, but the problem with them is surface stitches leave large needle holes.

Inkjet-printable fabrics are soft and flexible and can be sewn on like any other fabric. I like using existing fabrics and "painting them in," but I also want to thread paint other beautiful images that are not on ready-made fabric. Now, I can get those "paintings" onto fabric to thread paint any image. I hope that you will learn this technique and make it your own. Add your own innovations, and use your own images to make your work unique.

Contents

Before You Begin

Thread painting requires some basic tools and supplies. Take a minute to look through this section for an overview of the materials you will need. Most of these items are easy to find, but if your local fabric store doesn't carry them, check the resource list in the back of the book.

Tools of the Trade

Here are some basic tools and supplies you might find helpful for thread sketching and painting:

- Sewing machine
- Darning foot
- Variety of sewing machine needles
- Threads in a variety of colors and types
- Rotary cutter
- Cutting mat
- Rotary ruler
- Scissors
- Seam ripper
- Stiletto
- Quilters' gloves
- Embroidery hoops
- Batting

- Inkjet-printable fabric
- Inkjet-printable tear-away stabilizer (foundation) papers
- Inkjet-printable wash-away stabilizer (foundation) papers
- Iron and ironing board
- Computer
- Inkjet printer
- Scanner
- Digital camera

Stabilizers

The easiest way to get your thread sketch onto fabric is to use inkjet-printable stabilizers. These products can also be put through a commercial copy machine so you can still use them even if you do not own a computer. There are two stabilizer types: tear-away and wash-away. Both have their place in thread sketching, and will be discussed in detail later. It is nice to keep a supply of both on hand.

Inkjet-Printable Fabric

What it is

This product is key to the simple thread-painting techniques described in this book. Inkjet-printable fabric, available from several different manufacturers, is treated to accept ink from an inkjet printer and it is backed with paper to feed through the printer. After the image is printed, the paper backing is peeled off leaving a soft fabric that can be sewn, washed and ironed. These fabrics are designed specifically for use with inkjet printers, and will not work with laser printers.

What it isn't

The thread painting technique taught in this book utilizes commercially available inkjet-printable fabrics. It is important to distinguish between this and heatset products that work well for many applications, but are not recommended for this technique.

There are two types of heat-set transfers — one for inkjet printers and one for commercial copiers. Both of these products involve printing a mirror-imaged photograph onto a transfer sheet, placing the transfer face down onto fabric, heat setting and peeling off the paper. This is fine for many applications, but the resulting fabric surface is thick, tacky and can not be sewn on without visible needle holes, making it inappropriate or thread painting.

Bubble Jet Set 2000

"Bubble Jet Set 2000" is a liquid for soaking cotton or silk fabrics, allowing them to be printable on an inkjet printer. The treated and dried fabric is ironed onto freezer paper so it can feed through a printer. After printing and removing the paper, the fabric is rinsed in "Bubble Jet Rinse." Although many quilters find this a more economical way to print fabrics, it is time consuming and the fabric can jam in the printer. It also has a short shelf life after it is prepared. Careful storage is needed to keep it printer-ready; commercially prepared fabric has no shelf life and can be used at a moment's notice.

Batting

Thread painting and sketching can be done with or without batting. Although fiber content does not make a difference, a thin batting works best. A good choice is batting sold by the yard. To avoid pinning, fusible batting is also recommended. Batting used while thread painting will help prevent distortion and it provides some stabilization.

Embroidery Hoops

For some projects, it is helpful to use an embroidery hoop. For thread painting and thread sketching, I prefer a spring-tension plastic hoop that fits under the darning foot. A 7" circular hoop is an ideal size to get started, although many sizes and shapes are available.

Other Goodies

Some people find **quilters' gloves** helpful when doing free-motion stitching. These thin cotton gloves with rubber grippers on the fingertips can be helpful when moving the fabric around, especially for quilters with carpal tunnel or arthritis.

A **stiletto** is also useful. This inexpensive tool looks like a miniature ice pick. It is helpful for pulling up bobbin thread, holding pieces in place while snipping threads, holding fabric in place while painting and guiding thicknesses of batting and fabric under the foot while sewing.

A **seam ripper** is convenient to score stabilizer for removal.

Digital Camera

This is my favorite toy, and I find it's a wonderful tool for snapping photos for thread paintings from the things I see around me daily. I carry mine around all the time, just in case I see the perfect thread painting in the course of my day — many of the photos used in the featured quilts were shot this way. Don't worry if you do not have a digital camera, there are lots of places to find fantastic images for thread painting.

Computer Equipment

Like a digital camera, a computer is great for thread painting, but not essential. I use mine to download pictures, store digital images and manipulate photographs in Adobe Photoshop. I use a scanner to copy images from books. If you do not have a computer,

or if your printer does not print good-quality color images, you can still learn to thread paint using this technique. You can use this technique directly on commercially available fabric.

Sewing Machine Basics

Machine Checkups

Lint and dust build up in the bobbin area of the machine, and this alone can affect tension settings. It is important to periodically check the bobbin area and clean out any dust and lint, following the guidelines in your owner's manual. One burst of canned air can be used to clean out the bobbin area each time the bobbin is changed.

Just like a car, a sewing machine responds well to a yearly tune-up to keep it running smoothly. I always take mine in the week of my birthday, an easy way to remember.

Darning Foot

For normal sewing, the function of a presser foot is to hold the fabric down firmly so that the feed dogs can pull it through the machine. For free-motion sewing, the foot needs to float over the fabric surface so that you can move the fabric freely. Since both thread sketching and thread painting are a variation of free-motion stitching, a darning foot is of utmost importance.

Look for a clear plastic darning foot or one with a large opening for good visibility. Check with your dealer for a darning foot designed specifically for your machine, or use a generic foot with a shank length to fit. The shank length is the distance from the attachment point to the actual foot. Shanks are high, low or slanted. If you are not sure which one your machine needs, unscrew the shank and presser foot and take them with you to the store.

Thread Tension

Sewing machine thread tension is often confusing, but it is important to understand how it works.

Perfectly balanced tension means that the needle thread and the bobbin thread meet in the middle of the fabric.

Well-balanced tension looks even on the front and the back of the fabric.

If the top tension is too tight (too high a number), the bobbin thread will be pulled to the surface.

When the tension is too high, the bobbin thread shows on the fabric surface.

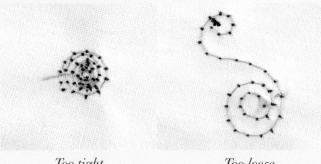

Too tight   *Too loose*

If the top tension is too loose (too low a number), the needle thread will be pulled to the fabric underside. Remember it this way: "If the bobbin thread comes up, turn the number down."

Machines with self-adjusting tension rarely need to be adjusted, although sometimes a manual override is necessary.

Before adjusting tension, always make note of the starting number. Make changes in small increments, and test-stitch each time until you achieve a balanced stitch. Test tension using a different thread color in the bobbin and the needle, so that it is obvious if there is an imbalance. Know your machine, and keep notes about which tension settings look best and with which threads.

Mixing different thread types between the bobbin and needle can also affect tension. Some machines need a lower tension setting to accommodate metallics and monofilament threads. Many decorative threads also require a lower tension setting. Depending on your particular machine, tension may need to be reduced to a setting as low as No. 1.

Changing fabrics and/or battings can also necessitate a change in tension. A good rule of thumb: for any factor that changes, recheck the tension. Changing the tension setting a small amount can make a big difference in stitch quality. Ironically, when logic suggests turning the number down, the reverse can sometimes produce a better result.

Some books recommend making adjustments to the bobbin tension. If your machine has a separate bobbin case (not built-in), there is a small screw on the side to adjust tension. It is my opinion that adjustments to the bobbin case are not a good idea. This is a very delicate adjustment, and once changed it is often difficult to return it to the original position. Most tension problems can be solved by making changes to the upper tension. If you suspect that the bobbin tension needs adjustment, seek assistance from a repair technician. If you do feel you need to adjust the bobbin tension for certain sewing situations, buy a second case and mark it with nail polish so it's easily distinguishable from your regular bobbin case.

On some machines there is a small hole in the bobbin case finger and the bobbin thread can be guided through this hole before coming up through the needle plate, which allows the thread to sit on the fabric surface. I find this makes a huge difference in the overall look of the final thread painting. Check your owner's manual to see if your machine has a similar feature.

Thread

Think of thread as your paint box, and start with an assortment of small spools in colors you like. Any thread designed for machine sewing will work for thread painting; different types of threads produce different effects, and various thread types can easily be combined within a single project. Having a wide selection on hand will ensure that you always have what you want while "painting."

Compare 30-wt. rayon, trilobal polyester and Dual Duty Plus threads on the same stitched designs.

Metallic, glitter and clear threads add sparkle.

It is helpful to have white, black and gray in either a polyester or polyester/cotton blend for the bobbin and a variety of colors to play with for the top. If you've never tried metallic or holographic threads, buy a spool of each and start playing! Once you get going with thread painting, you'll build a collection of wonderful colors to play with.

Threads come in a wide range of sizes; most general sewing threads are 30, 40 and 50, which refer to their weight. The lower the number, the thicker the thread.

Cotton threads lay down color that is relatively flat and uninteresting. This may not be the best choice for thread painting, but it may have its place in specific projects.

Polyester, or threads that contain polyester, have more sheen and thus more surface interest than those that are 100 percent cotton. Good-quality polyester threads are available in many colors, and allow a thinner line of stitching with a nice sheen when used in the needle. I also recommend them for use in the bobbin, regardless of the thread being used on top of the machine.

Polyester.

Trilobal polyester is a relative newcomer to the thread scene, and not available everywhere. It is strong, colorfast, and has even more sheen than regular polyester, which makes it an interesting choice for thread painting. Like rayon in appearance, trilobal polyester threads are washable and more durable than rayons.

Trilobal polyester.

Cotton-wrapped polyester thread, like Coats and Clark Dual Duty, gives the strength and durability of cotton, with the sheen of polyester. It is slightly thicker than most 100 percent polyester threads, comes in many colors and is reasonably priced. Widely available, and appropriate for all types of sewing and quilting, it's available in small spools, making it easy to purchase lots of colors to build a palette. It is also a good choice for bobbin thread.

Cotton-wrapped polyester.

Rayon thread has a beautiful sheen to it, but it isn't as colorfast as polyester, and also not as strong. It should only be used for decorative surface stitching, never for construction. The middle range of rayon thread colors have the most beautiful sheen. Heavier weights of rayon thread fill in much quicker than lighter weight threads. However, if you want color to come through from the image underneath, heavyweight threads tend to obscure it.

Rayon.

Metallic threads are wonderful for adding a bit of sparkle to your work. Think beyond silver and gold — metallics now come in a wide range of beautiful colors from a variety of manufacturers. A little goes a long way, and metallics are most effective when used in small amounts. When using metallic thread, a metallic needle is required. Metallic needles have a larger eye so the thread slides through smoothly. Some metallic threads are constructed by spiraling metallic fibers around a polyester core, and if used with a regular sewing needle, the metallic wrapping may get stripped, or the thread may snag and break. Often metallic threads require a looser upper tension.

Even machines with automatic tension sometimes require a manual override when using metallic threads. Start with the tension set for regular sewing, but if that isn't working, jump to No. 1 and move in small increments from there. Stitch slowly and carefully to avoid damaging or breaking delicate metallic threads.

This thread is metallic.

Glitter threads do not look significantly different from metallics on the spool, but they are vastly different. Often called hologram or holographic threads, they have a luminesce quality, as they are highly reflective. Glitter threads can be washed, and pressed with low heat. Like metallic, a little goes a long way. If you only buy one glitter thread, buy clear (sometimes called crystal or pearl) to add iridescent sparkle without adding color.

This thread is glitter.

Monofilament threads are designed for invisible quilting. They are available in clear for most fabric colors, and smoke, which is non-reflective, for dark fabrics. In thread painting, clear monofilament thread can also be used to fill in an area with thread texture when the right color is not available. Smoke can add a slight shadow effect.

Variegated threads are comprised of a series of colors that change at either regular or irregular intervals, and are not recommended for thread painting. It is impossible to control where these colors fall in the design and it is better to use separate colors and direct their placement.

Try a variety of threads in your sewing machine, as each machine will handle the threads differently. Play with needles, tensions and stitches until you get the results you like.

Thread does deteriorate over time, and more quickly if exposed to light, so store your threads in a container or drawer away from light. To test a thread, unwind about eight inches and tug. If it breaks easily, it is no good and should be thrown away. If it breaks in your hand, it will certainly break while running through the sewing machine and this will only lead to frustration.

Good-quality thread is still the least expensive element of any sewing project, so it always pays to buy name brand, first-quality threads.

The position in which the thread sits on the sewing machine can also affect results. Threads on a cone are designed to sit horizontally, and threads on a spool are designed to sit vertically. Try each in both positions to determine which way the thread runs through the machine more smoothly without breaking.

Bobbin Thread

Before starting a thread painting project, wind several bobbins for quick and easy replacement. Anyone who sews knows that the bobbin always runs out one inch before the end of the last seam! For most thread painting projects, only three bobbin thread colors are usually necessary — white, black and gray. Polyester thread is a good choice for bobbins, regardless of which thread is used on the surface. It's thin and flexible, which not only allows more thread to fit onto the bobbin (making it last longer before rewinding) but it is also less likely to build up dust and lint in your machine. It is not necessary to use the same type of thread in the bobbin as on the top, although the sizes should be comparable.

White bobbin thread is used with light colors, or "clean clear colors" to keep them from looking muddy.

Black bobbin thread is essential for black or any dark color upper thread. If black is used in the bobbin with a light color top thread, it will make the color look dark and dull.

Medium gray in the bobbin is good for any color that is "dusty" or mid-tone. Gray in the bobbin will make black on the surface appear not quite so stark.

If adjusting the tension does not prevent the bobbin color from showing, consider winding a bobbin of the top color; or using clear monofilament thread in the bobbin.

Bobbin thread can be used to create an effect I call "tweeding," which combines a small amount of the bobbin color mixed into the surface color. To allow the bobbin color to pop to the surface, turn the tension dial to a higher number. The smaller the stitches, the more often the bobbin color will appear on the surface.

Needles

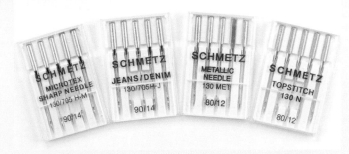

Sometimes, the success of any sewing project lies in using the right needle. In most cases for thread painting and sketching, an 80/12 sharp needle is the right choice. A size 90/14 is handy for thicker threads, a metallic needle is essential for use with metallic threads, and a topstitch needle is necessary for sketching with multiple threads.

What sometimes appears to be a bobbin or tension problem can actually be a needle problem. If the needle isn't correct for the fabric and/or thread being used, or if it's dull or has a burr, it may create stitching problems that mimic tension concerns. Often when a stitching problem arises, simply changing the needle will resolve it. A sewing machine needle should be changed after about four hours of sewing.

Changing a needle is simple. Loosen the needle screw — it is not necessary to remove the screw completely. Slide the needle down and out. Most machine needle shanks have one rounded and one flat side. In most cases the flat portion goes in the back. Gently push the new needle snugly into the clamp, and then tighten the screw.

Always make sure that the needle is appropriate for the fabric being sewn. Woven fabrics require a sharp needle, while knits require a ballpoint needle. They are not interchangeable. For thread painting and sketching, most often the fabric will be woven cotton which always requires a sharp needle.

Needles come in different sizes, and it is important to match the right size to the fabric and thread being used. Needle sizes are written as two numbers with a slash between them. The first number is the European needle size and the second is the American size. An 80/12 sharp is recommended for cotton. A heavier thread requires a larger needle, like 90/14.

Like many sewing supplies, a good-quality needle will not cost significantly more than a lesser quality one, but it can make a big difference in the stitch quality.

If you have difficulty threading a needle, cut the thread end at an angle just before threading. This makes a tiny point that is easier to thread than the flat edge that results from cutting the thread straight across. Do not put the end of the thread in your mouth; this causes the thread fibers to expand, making it even more difficult to get through the needle eye. If you still have trouble threading the needle, a topstitch needle has a larger eye, making it easier to thread, and the needle size is still appropriate for thread painting.

Techniques

Now that you know what materials you need, it is time to learn the techniques of free-motion stitching and thread sketching, lettering and thread painting. Then you will be ready to stitch your own beautiful works of original art!

Free-Motion Stitching

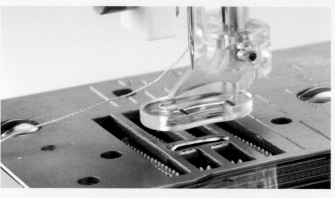

Lower the feed dogs for free-motion work.

The feed dogs are the jagged teeth that pull the fabric straight through the sewing machine. To begin free-motion stitching, the feed dogs must be dropped below the surface of the throat plate (the metal area in which they sit). Most machines have a button or lever to lower the feed dogs; others have a plate that fits over them. If your machine doesn't have a way to lower or cover the feed dogs, simply set the stitch length to zero. Consult your owner's manual for more information; feed dog adjustment is usually described under "darning." By disengaging the feed dogs, the machine will only stitch in place, and you will move the fabric.

Many quilters insist that free-motion sewing can be done with the feed dogs in the up position. I have certainly done this inadvertently many times, and it will not damage the sewing machine. However, it will make free-motion stitching more difficult. Either way, it is important that the darning foot is positioned to float over the fabric surface. This may mean manually loosening the amount of presser foot pressure.

To begin free-motion stitching, position a piece of fabric backed with batting under the darning foot.

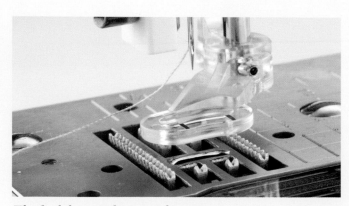

The feed dogs up for normal sewing.

Use the handwheel to lower the needle point into the fabric at your starting point. While holding the needle thread in your left hand, turn the handwheel forward with your right hand until the needle comes up out of the fabric. This pulls a loop of bobbin thread up with it. Using the point of a seam ripper, a pin, stiletto or small scissors, pull the bobbin thread loop up from the bottom so that both threads are now on the surface.

Holding both threads off to the left, take several stitches in place to lock the stitches, and after sewing a few more stitches, cut both threads off at the fabric surface. This process prevents "bird nesting" or thread clumping on the underside of your work.

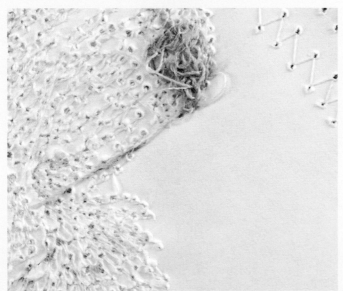

Bird nesting makes the underside of your work look messy.

Run the machine at a steady speed, move the fabric with your hands and the stitches will go in that direction. It is this coordination that sometimes takes some practice to reach the "ah ha" moment, when the machine speed and the hand movement feel like they are in sync. Moving the fabric too slowly will result in stitches that are too small and look like dots rather than stitches; moving it too fast will result in large, loopy stitches that may not hold. The goal is to create stitches that resemble the standard stitch length on your sewing machine. It does not matter what setting your stitch length is on, as **you** determine the stitch length simply by the speed at which you sew — faster equals bigger stitches.

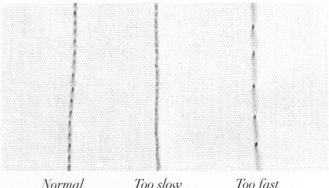

Normal   *Too slow*   *Too fast*

The more free-motion stitching you do, the more proficient you will become. It is easiest to learn in larger areas making large sweeping lines, as small areas and tight curves require more control. Many people find the use of quilters' gloves or rubber fingertips helpful in grasping the fabric and moving it smoothly.

At the end of a "line" of stitching, make several stitches in place again before removing the fabric from the sewing machine and cutting off the threads. Simply hold the fabric in place for three or four stitches. Some machines have a lock stitch or "fix" feature that will do the same thing.

Keep your shoulders relaxed and knees and elbows bent at a 90-degree angle to the work surface when you stitch to prevent fatigue. Stop every 15 minutes to stretch.

Practice on scrap fabric with batting underneath (no need for another fabric layer on the bottom, as the feed dogs in their down position cannot catch the batting) until the coordination feels fluid and effortless. Relax and "go with the flow."

Learning to coordinate the machine speed and the speed at which you move your hands is the hard part of free-motion sewing. The good news is that in thread painting, the length of stitches is not as critical as it is in free-motion quilting, so you don't need to be an expert to get started.

Thread Sketching

Choosing an Image

To begin, choose a design with simple lines. One good source for simple line drawings is children's coloring books. Once you become proficient at thread sketching, pen-and-ink drawings and even photographs are a wonderful source of inspiration. As you learn to thread sketch, keep in mind that large shapes with big curves are easier to sketch than little designs with lots of tiny curves. Also, the original design will be torn or dissolved away, so if the thread does not stay exactly on the lines, no one will ever know.

Remember, when the feed dogs are down, the stitch length is determined solely by your movement of the fabric.

Transferring the Image to Fabric

It is not necessary to know how to draw, as there are several ways to transfer any drawing to fabric for thread sketching.

When using a light-color fabric, it is possible to simply trace the design onto the fabric using a mechanical pencil. This leaves a very thin line that can be washed out. For simple designs, use a light box or tape the design and the fabric to a window to make the design easier to trace. This works well when the design is not very complicated, but when it is, it can be very time-consuming.

Choosing the Right Stabilizer

For more complex designs, rather than tracing, there is an easier way to get the design onto fabric — inkjet-printable stabilizer paper (foundation paper). Print the design directly onto the stabilizer and pin it to the top of the fabric.

The thread sketching is created by stitching along the lines printed on the stabilizer. When the stitching is complete, the stabilizer is removed.

One advantage of using this paper method is that images can be re-sized either in the computer or by enlarging or reducing on a copy machine, and they can be printed in multiples. When using a computer graphics program, the image can even be stretched and modified, allowing total flexibility.

There are two types of these printable stabilizers: tear-away and wash-away, and although they accomplish the same task, there are times when one is preferred over the other.

Tear-away is a good choice for designs that have large blank areas that allow it to be easily torn away from the stitching. To remove it, use the back of a seam ripper, score the stitch line and the stabilizer will tear away easily from the stitches.

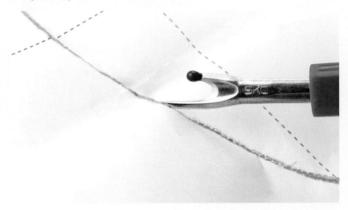

To avoid pulling on the stitches, place your fingernail on the stitching line when tearing. The tip of a straight pin is a useful tool to "pop" the pieces of the stabilizer out from between stitches. For little pieces that remain stuck under the stitches, scratch lightly with your fingernail to loosen them.

In a pinch, regular computer or typing paper can do the same job as tear-away stabilizer. The difference is that it is more difficult to remove and will dull the needle more quickly. If you use regular paper, scoring and holding the stitches with your fingernail while tearing the paper away is even more important.

For more complex designs with many tiny areas that would be too difficult or time-consuming to pop out, use a wash-away stabilizer. This product is slightly more expensive than tear-away, but it is the easiest way to remove stabilizer from hard-to-access areas. Although the stabilizer is dissolvable, the ink is not, so print designs in gray or in the thread color, and use "draft" mode to reduce the amount of ink used. When the stitching is complete, tear away any large areas of stabilizer, and soak the piece following the manufacturer's instructions for removal. Rub gently with either an old toothbrush, or sea sponge (available from most paint stores) to remove stabilizer caught between stitches. Use a small amount of dish soap or wash the project gently and thoroughly to dissolve any remaining stabilizer.

Thread sketches need not be limited to the size of the stabilizer paper. Small designs can be printed onto one or more sheets, cut apart and applied to different areas of a project. If the desired thread sketch is larger than the stabilizer sheet, print it in sections and tape together. It is not crucial to have every line match up exactly, as that adjustment can easily be made while stitching. Try to keep the tape away from the stitching lines. On wash-away stabilizer, pull off any tape before dissolving.

Selecting Fabric

Choose a base fabric that is a solid color or one that reads like a solid so that the thread work will show.

Select threads and fabric with high contrast for maximum impact — dark thread on light fabric or light thread on dark fabric.

Sewing With Multiple Threads

Thread choice can make a big difference in the finished appearance of your thread sketch. The thicker the thread, the heavier the lines of the drawing — much like the difference between using a fine- or thick-point marker. It is possible to use multiple strands of fine thread together, as if they were a single strand, for a thicker stitch line.

To use multiple threads, wind two or three bobbins with the same color. Stack the bobbins on the machine's spool pin with the thread feeding off in the same direction. On some sewing machines both threads can be threaded through the machine at one time; on others they need to feed separately. Experimenting with your machine will determine which way works best to pull the threads through the upper tension. A topstitching needle allows easy threading of multiple strands because of its larger eye.

22

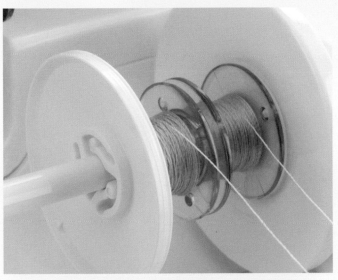

Start Sketching

To position the printed design on your fabric, fold your fabric in half vertically and horizontally and press gently, either with an iron or your fingers. This leaves a light foldline through the centers. Fold the design the same way and match up the fold lines. Pin the printed stabilizer pattern to the right side of the fabric. Avoid putting pins on the lines that will be stitched.

Thread sketching can be done either on fabric with batting underneath, or on the fabric alone. The addition of batting allows the stitches to sink into the fabric, creating dimension. Without batting, the thread sits on the fabric surface. This is a personal preference, or is often determined by the final use of the thread sketch.

Lightweight batting adds dimension to the thread sketch.

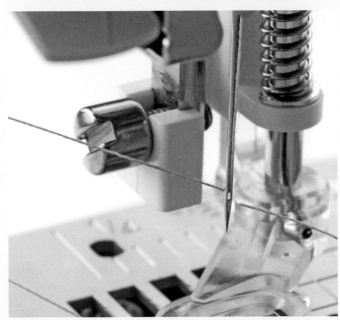

Thread the needle one thread at a time, holding the strands already through the eye toward the top, so the next one can easily slide through at the bottom.

When doubling or tripling the thread, the tension must be adjusted to accommodate the extra thickness. Even on machines with self-adjusting tension, start at No. 1 and adjust from there. If there are thread loops on the underside of your test sample, or if the threads are breaking, adjust the tension. Aim for a normal looking stitch on the front and back of the work.

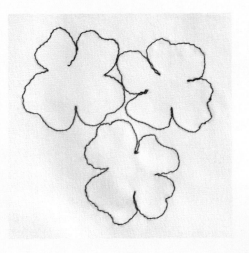

Without batting, the sketching sits on the surface of the fabric.

If batting is not used, it may be helpful to hoop the fabric. This prevents puckering, and it helps maintain the fabric's size and shape.

If the thread sketch is fairly simple, the printed stabilizer is often enough to keep the fabric stable. Otherwise, pin another piece of the stabilizer under the fabric and tear it away after the stitching is complete — this will stabilize the fabric without using a hoop. Using a darning foot, position the fabric under the needle, and lower the feed dogs. Pull the bobbin thread to the surface and hold it off to the side while making a lock stitch. Cut the trailing threads away to prevent bird nesting. Stitch slowly and carefully, following the design lines. Maintain an even machine speed, and move the fabric smoothly for an even stitch length. A needle-down function is very helpful when stopping and/or turning the work, allowing for cleaner corners and even stitches.

When starting and stopping any line of stitching, remember to lock the stitches, both at the beginning and at the end, or the threads will pull out. A continuous-line drawing can be stitched with only one starting and stopping point. Designs that are not one continuous line require a lock stitch every time the needle moves to another area. To jump to another area of the design, simply lock the stitches, lift the foot, and pull the needle to the new starting place. Begin again with another lock stitch. This creates a jump stitch that will be trimmed later on both sides of the fabric. There is no need to pull your work out of the machine after every line of stitching.

Because the feed dogs are not engaged, you can stitch in any direction. That means forward, backward or sideways. Continuously turn the fabric, as needed, to see the lines and for personal comfort. I always find it easiest to stitch toward me.

For areas of the sketch that will be filled in with thread, make the outline, remove the top stabilizer and then fill in the area with stitches.

After all the stitching is complete, remove the stabilizer and press the fabric. Be careful not to iron back and forth, but press gently up and down to allow the threads to relax into the fabric. Placing a towel on the ironing surface helps prevent puckering.

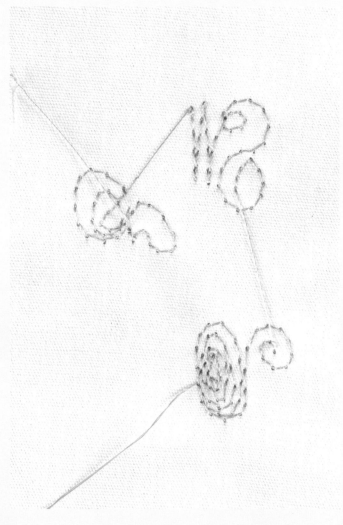

Lettering

Lettering is no different than sketching, and any kind of lettering can be done using this technique. Choose a computer font, your own handwriting, or even a child's handwriting and print the desired size onto tear-away stabilizer. Pin to the right side of the fabric and follow the outlines of the letters using free-motion stitching.

Remove the stabilizer, leaving only the lettering outlines.

Use short back-and-forth strokes to fill in between the outlines.

For lettering that sits on the fabric surface, stitch it without batting. For lettering that looks recessed into a puffy surface, stitch the lettering with batting behind the fabric.

If you are filling in large areas without batting underneath, use a hoop. Remember, lettering on a quilt must be done before assembling or you will have mirror writing on the quilt back.

This is a wonderful way to add personal messages to quilts, pillows and garments. It's also a great way to make personalized quilt labels.

Thread Painting
Selecting Images

Not every photograph or painting is a good candidate for thread painting; some are much better than others. Look for simple artwork with clean lines and clear color distinction. Anything that is sketchy, has lots of brush strokes or other textured areas, will work well. Avoid very soft watercolors or other artwork where the colors and edges blur into each other, as this is very difficult to replicate with thread. Some lovely old paintings have indistinguishable dark areas that are difficult to follow with thread.

Working from a photo of a tapestry, embroidery or other textile works well, as there are clearly distinct color areas. Sketches, pen-and-ink drawings and pastels work well for the same reason. Nature photos and paintings translate beautifully into thread — the textures and colors in tree bark, flower petals, even water, look wonderful when thread painted. Landscapes can be good beginner projects. Flowers work especially well, since no flower is perfect, there are no mistakes.

Animals are a natural subject for thread painting, as thread brings texture to both fur and feathers.

A strong "focal point" in the artwork draws the viewer to look more closely. A focal point can fill the frame for maximum impact, or it can be set off to one side. For a more interesting and compelling composition, use the one-third and two-thirds rule. A seascape, for example, will look better if it is one-third sky and two-thirds beach (or one-third beach and two-thirds sky) rather than splitting the scene into equal halves. Crop pictures to eliminate distracting backgrounds. Choose a close-up of an animal face, for instance, rather than a distant shot with a lot of background.

A scene with elements evenly divided results in a composition that looks dull.

The same scene with the elements split in thirds makes a more appealing composition.

The artwork you have in mind is a good candidate for thread painting if:

- lines can be easily followed
- colors can be clearly distinguished
- there is good contrast — light and dark areas
- there are no conflicting elements in the background
- detail is compatible with your thread painting skill
- there is a strong focal point
- there are no large flat areas of color that may not look right as a stitched texture
- the image you are choosing is the same style as your project

After selecting an image, scan it into the computer, upload from a digital camera, or download from the Internet. If you have computer software that allows you to alter an image, lighten the original artwork and increase the contrast (this can also be accomplished on some printers). Remember, the image does not translate onto the printable fabric exactly as it looks on the screen. Colors on a computer screen are not always the same when printed. Play with color balance and preview on paper until you like the way the image looks.

One common adjustment for fabric printing is increased saturation. Another is to alter the color balance cooler (toward blue on the scale) or warmer (toward red). The design is covered with stitching so nothing is critical. Usually, I just lighten the image and increase the contrast.

Programs like Adobe Photoshop or Adobe Photoshop Elements are very useful in manipulating photographs for better thread paintings, lines can be softened, colors deepened or changed, contrast increased or the image can be cropped for more impact. Experienced program users can manipulate the photograph by cutting and pasting elements, and eliminating areas of the photo that may be distracting.

Many commercially printed fabrics offer a panel or repeat that makes a nice composition for a thread painting.

Copyright

If an art quilt is for your personal use, kept in your home and shared with your family and friends, copyright infringement is not a concern. However, if you want to exhibit the quilt publicly, enter it in a quilt show, feature it in a magazine, book or newspaper, or sell it, then copyright becomes an important issue.

Every artist or photographer owns the right to his/her work, and these images cannot be used without consent. Even if only a small section of the image is used, or if the image is substantially altered, it is still protected by copyright. Copyright is in effect even if the artist does not register it, and it remains in effect until 70 years after the artist's death. At that time the work passes into the public domain, meaning it can be used without permission, although there are still exceptions.

Well-known images like famous cartoon characters, or any recognizable images of people, are copyright protected and cannot ever be reproduced without permission. Photos that appear on the Internet are also protected by copyright. In many cases, museums hold a copyright on a particular photograph of a work, even if the work itself is in the public domain.

The rule of thumb for copyright questions — if in doubt, check it out!

There are many sources for artwork that are in the public domain. Many Web sites have public domain images. Any photos in the archives of the U.S. Government, like the National Fish and Wildlife Service, NASA, and other government agencies, can be used freely. The works of artists who are long gone (like Cézanne, Van Gogh and Rembrandt) are generally in the public domain (although some of the photos from the museums that house them are not). One reason the Mona Lisa is so often reproduced is that there is no longer any copyright concern.

For personal use, look at the Web sites of major museums. Many contain database photos from their

collections that can be downloaded. Art books are also a wonderful source of beautiful images perfect for thread painting.

If the art piece will hang in your home, the quilt police will not come and arrest you! But for anything that may be shown in public or sold, be very careful about the images you use. Always ask permission first!

Think first about photographs taken by your family and friends, or your own photos. Children's artwork also makes charming thread paintings.

Using Inkjet-Printable Fabrics

There are several brands of pre-backed inkjet-printable fabrics ready to use. For this technique, white cotton poplin works very well. Once the image is determined, examine the fabric sheet. Remove any loose threads

or lint on the fabric surface as they will leave an area unprinted. Trim any long threads around the edges to avoid printer jams. Load a single fabric sheet into the printer so the image will print on the fabric side.

The print quality is only as good as the printer; horizontal banding or other printer problems will appear on the fabric the same way they appear on paper. If banding occurs on paper prints, clean the printer heads or change the ink cartridge before printing on fabric.

For most printable fabrics, there is no need to use a "high-quality" print setting, the normal setting works fine. Follow the specific instructions for the particular brand you are using. Some printers require a "heavy-weight paper" setting to feed fabric sheets. (Check in the printer properties box on your computer.)

After printing, let it sit for a few minutes until it's completely dry (the time will vary by printer and by product). Remove the paper backing by carefully rolling it off the back of the fabric. Yanking one corner and pulling diagonally will result in distortion.

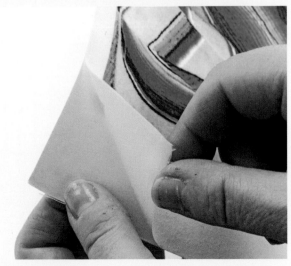

If the fabric becomes distorted while removing the paper backing, place it flat and coax it into shape. Some fabric brands recommend rinsing to remove excess ink, or heat-setting; check the manufacturer's directions. If you do rinse, air dry on a towel or place the fabric in a microwave for about a minute for faster drying.

Using Fabric

Another easy way to start thread painting is to use commercially printed fabric and "paint it in." Many fabrics on the market today are as beautiful as artwork. Look for Asian-inspired fabrics, large florals, and fabrics with animals, plants or novelty motifs. Many fabrics are designed to be used as panels — a perfect canvas for thread painting.

Another advantage of using commercial fabric as a base for thread painting is that the same fabric can be used elsewhere in the project, for a custom look.

Using fabric is also an easy way to choose thread colors, as most fabrics have a printing key on the selvage. Look for a series of circles or squares on one selvage showing every color used in production. Match thread colors, or go a shade lighter or darker.

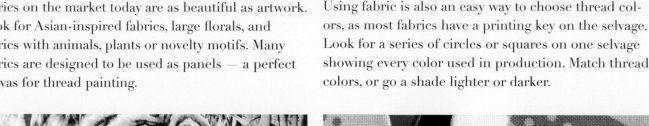

Not all areas of the design need to be totally covered in thread. The purpose of thread painting is to add texture and brighten the color, and this can be achieved by choosing some areas to "paint" with thread and leaving others plain.

One of the advantages of using printed fabric is the design and color clarity. Look closely at the fabric you are considering and you can probably see where one color blends into another with fine lines — easy to duplicate with thread. Often there are metallic accents on the fabric which can be painted with metallic thread.

The dragonfly fabric shown below illustrates how thread can be used to accent the flower petals, without covering the entire printed area. This gives the flower petals more impact. The petals can also be filled in completely, giving them more of an embroidered look. Notice that the color of the dragonfly has been changed. In the original fabric the dragonfly is maroon, but I wanted it to be more bright and lively, so I used red thread. By lightly thread painting, the maroon still shows through. I also used the gold printing on the fabric as a guide for a bit of metallic thread. I didn't feel the same was needed on the flowers; a bit of sparkle made the dragonflies the focal point.

In the flower petals, I used two similar colors, the darker one in the bottom center of each petal (following the colors put there by the fabric artist) and then a second slightly lighter color used only at the tip of the first color. The result is a subtle blending of color that is much like the airbrushing of the original fabric design.

Now, you can look at fabric differently. Just one repeat of a design will make a beautiful thread painting, giving stash fabrics and fat quarters a whole new life.

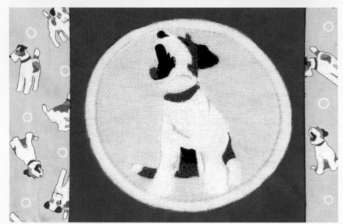

Another way to use existing fabric is to scan it and print it onto the inkjet-printable fabric. This allows you to use a motif you like, but that needs to be resized. The dogs on this fabric were too small to be thread painted, so each one was scanned and enlarged, printed and thread painted. When scanning fabric, use a low resolution setting, (around 300 dpi). Although logic would tell you that the higher the dpi the clearer the image, it will also clearly copy the weave of the fabric. (Be sure to read "Copyright" on page 28 before scanning and using commercially printed fabrics.)

To Hoop or Not to Hoop

Although a hoop isn't necessary for free-motion quilting, using a hoop for thread painting can help maintain a flat, pucker-free surface. There are several types and sizes of hoops. Wooden hoops require tightening a screw to secure the inner and outer portions; spring-tension hoops snap into place. Although a thin 7"-diameter hoop serves most thread painting needs; hoops are fairly inexpensive, so I suggest having several kinds and sizes for convenience. It is important that no matter which kind of hoop you choose, it must fit under the darning foot.

To use an embroidery hoop, place the larger portion flat on a table. Cover it with the batting and fabric so the paintable area is centered. Position the inner hoop over the fabric and push it firmly in place. When using an adjustable hoop, tighten the screw to hold the fabric taut, but not so tight that it stretches out of shape. The fabric is in the hoop correctly if it sits flat against the sewing machine surface, (opposite from the traditional hand embroidery position). The hoop serves as a handle to make controlling the fabric easier and helps prevents bobbin thread from coming to the surface.

When hooping near a fabric edge, pin a scrap of fabric to the edge and use it to connect into the hoop.

If the thread painting is to be completed in several sewing sessions, remove the hoop between sessions. This will prevent fabric stretching and distortion.

Depending on the final use of the thread painting, paper can be used instead of a hoop. Because the paper on the back becomes a permanent part of the thread painting, it is not recommended for final functions that would require washing. But, for wall hangings, pillows, tote bags, even some garments, it works well. Place a sheet of stabilizer paper (or any paper without lines or markings) underneath the batting and pin into place. Now, you can work on the thread painting without using a hoop.

Choosing Thread Colors

Thread colors do not need to match the artwork colors exactly; in fact, the results are often better if they don't. A color that is close to, but not exactly the same when thread painted lightly, will give the illusion of more sophisticated shading, as the base color shows through. Often, when choosing thread colors, I identify the color in the artwork and buy two threads — one a shade lighter, and one a shade darker than the color in the art. I then use these alternately, allowing the original color to show through. The image printed onto fabric is just a starting point; colors can be changed, or even added, as the work progresses. Try adding colors that are not in the original artwork.

Stop periodically and examine your work; change the things you don't like.

Any color can be added anywhere you want.

Start Painting

I usually begin thread painting by filling in the focal point. Often I don't know until the thread painting develops exactly what and where certain colors will go, and how much or how little will be filled in with thread. Think about areas where one color clearly sits under another and thread paint accordingly. For example, leaves sit over a tree trunk meaning the trunk area should be "painted" before the leaves.

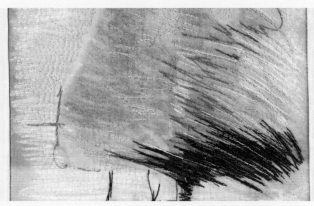

In most cases, the choice of starting color does not matter. You might find it easier to stitch one color wherever it will appear on the thread painting before going on to the next color. Or, you may choose to finish one section and evaluate before moving on.

Another option is to use all the colors with a particular bobbin color first, so that you do not need to continually change the bobbin thread. There are no absolute rules — find what works most comfortably for you.

Some people like to start with an outline of a shape and then fill it in; others like to begin filling in and end at the edges. (As children, we all had our own coloring "style" with crayons and thread painting is no different.)

A Step-by-Step Guide to Thread Painting

My friend, Peggy, took this snapshot of her cat, Frankie. As a snapshot it was fine, but for an art quilt it needed more drama. I cropped the photo so that all the focus was on the eyes — I loved the contrast of the black and white fur with the yellow eyes. When I told Peggy I wanted to use this in the book, she said when Frankie found out he was going to be famous, there would be no living with him! That is why this quilt is called "Frankie Hits the Big Time." Maybe there is a "Frankie" in your life — the instructions here are intended to illustrate the step-by-step process of completing a thread painting.

Construction

1. Make any adjustments to the photo and print it onto computer printable fabric.

2. Place photo onto thin batting (plain or fusible) and either back it with paper, or put in a hoop.

3. As the eyes are the focal point of this piece, and are close to the center of the image, it makes sense to start with them. With feed dogs down and darning foot on the machine, begin with the black area in the center of the eye. Start by pulling the bobbin thread to the surface and doing a lock stitch.

4. Because I wanted the eyes to be very dramatic, I took some liberties with the colors of the thread. I decided to use colors that were more yellow and brighter than the photo. The three colors I chose are very close to each other, but different enough to blend and create drama.

5. I started with the most orange of the colors, and used it around the black in the center of the eyes. (Note, when using black thread in the top of the machine, I used black thread in the bobbin; when using the yellow colors, there was white in the bobbin; for the gray thread — gray in the bobbin.)

6. Next, using the darkest of the yellow colors, outline the darker area of the eyes, following their shape.

7. Using the lightest yellow color, the remainder of the eye is filled in. It is important to remember the shape that is being thread painted; in this case the eye is round, and the color in an eye radiates out from the center. For that reason, the eye will look most natural if the thread goes in that direction—the final "fill-in" color is not painted straight back and forth, but radiates out from the center. Notice, too, how all the colors blend together, and how the color comes through from underneath — it does not need to be filled in densely. Trim any threads from the front and the back so that nothing will get caught when you move on.

9. The gray is next. Remember, it is not necessary to fill in the fur completely; it will have more dimension and be easier to do if it just loosely fills in with color. This is the advantage of this technique — color comes through from the print itself, allowing less thread work, and a look of depth. Don't forget that little spot that defines the mouth — it is a small detail that makes a big difference in the final thread painting.

8. Next, move on to the white fur. The white is the center of the image, so it is the next logical step. Remember to move the thread in the same direction as the fur; when the fur direction changes, so will the thread. Where the fur is tight and dense, like the nose, make the stitches tighter and denser — in areas where the fur is fluffier, the thread work can be looser and lines of thread farther apart. At this point, the light pink of the nose is also filled in.

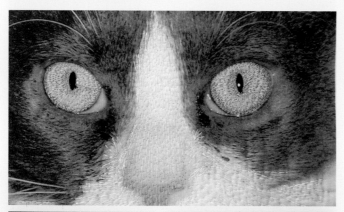

10. Now, move to the black thread. Too much would look too dense, so lightly fill in the black just for intensity of color and contrast. Step away and look at the piece periodically and ask yourself if it needs something, and where. Every person will approach this a little differently, but that is the way to add your personal touch. Remember, you are creating art! Look at how little black I actually added, and how much space is between lines of black thread.

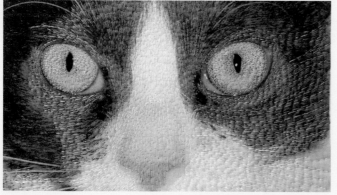

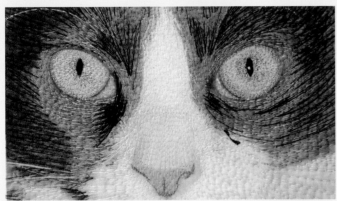

11. Look at the final piece and decide where you might want to do some detail work. Here, I used some darker pink to give the nose more definition; clear glitter thread livened up the white of the eyes, the reflective spot in the eyes, and the whiskers; and a little gold glitter thread added to the center of the eye brightened and gave the eyes some sparkle.

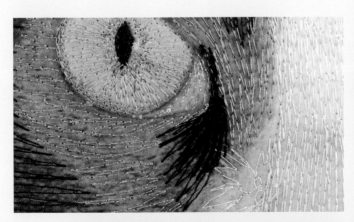

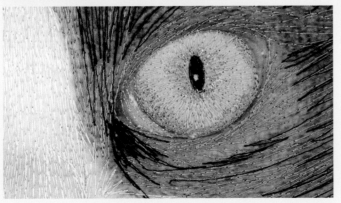

12. Bring the thread painting to a cutting board, and square it off.

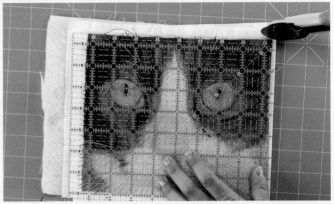

13. Add borders to complement your thread painting — I used two thin borders in the same yellow/orange tones as the thread I used for the eyes, and a wider black and white border to relate to the black and white of the cat's fur.

14. Layer with batting and backing fabric and quilt as you would with any other small quilt. I did free-motion quilting around the eyes and nose to hold the piece together, but also to give a little added dimension to those areas.

Contouring

Consider the shape being filled with stitches and move back and forth in an appropriate manner. If "painting" an apple, for example, curve the stitches as you move, imitating the apple's roundness. Grass or animal fur is best expressed with short spiky movements. Flower petals are stitched tightly together in the center and radiate outward with more space left between stitches. This gives your thread painting a more realistic texture.

Blending and Shading

Shading is accomplished by leaving a wider space between stitches, and filling that space in with a second color. To blend colors, extend the second color into and on top of the first color. Shading and blending can be done with many colors blending in a single area until it has the look you like. The thicker the thread, the more quickly an area will "fill in" with thread color, so thinner threads often work better for blending.

Sit Back...Take a Look...

Complete the main motif, changing colors and re-hooping as needed. Look at the work and re-evaluate periodically. Does it need more color in a certain place? Does it need more definition?

Contrast is key, and sometimes adding a dark thread color as an accent (or a light one) will make the design more pronounced and artistic. The printed image is only a starting point. Add a color that isn't there, change a color that is, blend several colors — the base artwork is only a guide. If there are areas that will not be thread painted (for example, a sky that will be stippled), do not stitch them at this point — it will be done when the thread painting is placed in the final project.

The goal of thread painting is to express your *own* artistic vision. Everyone who attempts the same image will create a different thread painting. Even if you stitch the same image again, it will not look exactly the same. Relax, have fun and make it your own. Don't get too focused on any one small area. The finished image will be viewed as a whole and every little stitch is not as important as the overall effect.

Finishing

Remove your masterpiece from the hoop, if you are using one, or remove any backing paper not stitched in place. Trim any stray threads and make sure it looks finished. Touch-ups done at this point do not necessarily need to be hooped; if the fabric surface is well covered with thread, it isn't likely to pucker.

When using a hoop, the original fabric shape may become distorted — the more surface thread, the greater the distortion. Gently press the piece with steam from the fabric side to avoid flattening or melting the batting. Press from the center to the outside edges to smooth away any hoop ridges. A press cloth will protect the surface of your work.

Place the finished thread painting on a cutting mat, and using a ruler and rotary cutter, trim the edges so that the corners are square and all sides are straight.

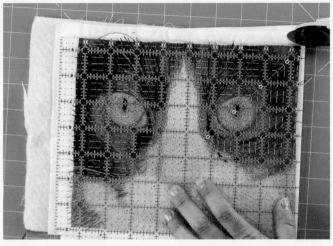

Blocking

Thread paintings can become distorted, not only from the use of a hoop, but from all the threads pulling the sides in. If the thread painting is truly distorted, it can be blocked, like a sweater, after washing. Pin the thread painting to an ironing board, gently pulling the four corners so that the piece is squared. I find that quilters' safety pins are stronger than straight pins, and can be put in like a straight pin, opened. First pin the upper and lower edges, then the two sides. Keep gently pulling the block into shape and putting pins in until the shape looks right. Mist it lightly with water (no need to get it really wet) and if it is particularly stubborn, pull and pin it again, as it will be more flexible when damp.

Allow the thread painting to dry completely while pinned, or dry with the use of a steam iron (protect the surface with a press cloth). Allow it to cool before removing the pins. When the pins are removed, the piece should no longer appear distorted.

Color Boosting

Inherent in the transfer of images from the computer to the printable fabric is some loss of color intensity. For the most part, color loss does not adversely affect the thread painting, as there will be thread over most of it. But, there are times when it can be a problem.

In this thread painting, the thread work is concentrated on the blanket.

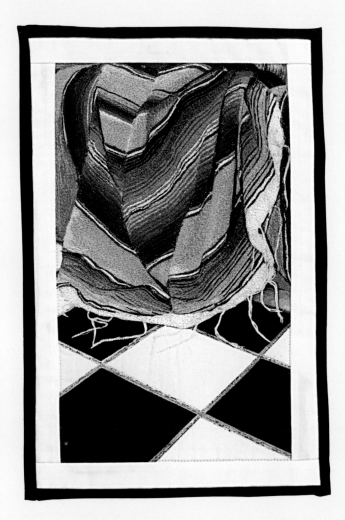

Filling in the floor tiles would not be advisable because of the thread texture. It also would take a long time and use lots of thread with minimal impact. But the black tiles did not appear black on the fabric, but dark gray. I helped this along with a little fabric paint. Using a small brush, I painted just the black tile areas, a detail that heightens the contrast of the floor, and gives more impact to the finished thread painting.

Fabric paints are widely available and come in a variety of colors. Fabric or textile medium can be added to any paint, allowing it to be used successfully on fabric. When a small amount is added to paint, it allows the paint to soak into the fabric without cracking or flaking as it might without the medium. Although it looks white, the medium does not change the paint color.

When using fabric paint, dip the brush lightly and brush any excess paint off onto a paper towel. This prevents saturating the fabric. If the paint seems thick, thin with a tiny amount of water so that there is only a light "film" of paint on the surface.

Pinning the fabric to an ironing board or taping to a table helps hold it in place while you paint. I find a stiletto useful to hold the fabric, as the brush sometimes tends to drag. If the thread painting has already been done, protect it with a piece of scrap fabric or paper so paint drips do not ruin all your hard work.

This dog fabric illustrates a similar problem. Although the dogs look wonderful as thread paintings, if they are to be used with the original fabric, the background is too light and appears pink rather than the red in the actual material. A small amount of strategically placed red paint in the background corrects this and makes it work well with the original fabric without filling the entire background with thread. Even though the red paint isn't exactly the same shade, it is close enough to relate to the original red in the fabric.

Thinking Big

What do you do when you want to produce a thread painting from printable fabric larger than 8½" x 11"? Inkjet-printable fabric is available in a variety of sizes and fabric types. It comes on rolls and also larger single sheets.

If your printer cannot handle larger sizes, you can print the image in sections. Most printers have a "tiling" mode which will divide the image. It is also possible to bring the image into a computer graphics program and split it into sections. Each section will fit onto an 8½" x 11" sheet of fabric.

Print portions of an image separately when your finished work is larger than one sheet of printable fabric.

44

Leave space for seam allowances to join the pieces together. After printing, carefully pin the panels together in sequence so all the appropriate areas line up. Press the seam allowance open to reduce bulk. The resulting piece can be thread painted the same way as a smaller sized piece. Thread painting can be used to help hide the seaming, so plan your work before you print. This may mean that the image will be broken up into unequal sections to allow for seams in areas that will be covered with heavy thread painting. Print as many sections as you need to create the desired size.

Another interesting way to create a large thread painting is to kaleidoscope a single image. Print the image twice, and then print two more in mirror image. By turning the pieces so that common sides meet, you create a kaleidoscope, turning even a simple photo into an art quilt. Be sure to try the images both ways, as turning the outside edges to the center will create a totally different design. Seam them together and don't worry about covering the seam lines with thread, as they become part of the overall design. The project on page 87 is done this way.

Thread Painting as Embroidery

Whether or not you own an embroidery machine, thread painting can be used to create the look of fine embroidery.

Start by choosing the image to be embroidered, resize if necessary, and print onto inkjet-printable fabric. To conserve fabric, put several small images on one sheet, but do not let them overlap.

You can also identify an area of commercial fabric that would make a nice embroidery.

Use a paper-backed fusible product and fuse to the wrong side of your "embroidery." Carefully cut out each design, position onto your project and fuse in place. Now, thread paint the design directly onto your project. Make sure your thread work extends slightly beyond the cut edges to prevent fraying.

Highlight fused motifs with thread stitching.

Completely cover the printed fabric with thread embroidery.

Quilting Your Artwork

You probably already know how to construct a quilt, but if not, there are many good books available that describe the process in detail. When thread painting or sketching is done on thin batting, it can be added to a quilt like any other block. (It may help to use a walking foot.)

It is important to quilt the thread sketch or thread painting to the rest of the quilt. Sky or background that was left without thread can be stippled or quilted, or the basic shapes can be traced in clear thread

A series of borders using fabrics and colors that complement your work will create a frame. Audition fabrics by placing them next to your thread painting to decide what you like. This is your artwork, there are no rules.

Quilting

Quilting is done using either a clear or colored thread. A walking foot is always recommended when doing straight quilting stitches. The easiest way to quilt the borders is to stitch in the ditch. Use the center mark on the presser foot to guide the way along the seamline; watching the needle is more difficult.

Free-motion quilting on the borders is another option, as described earlier in this book. Use a design that complements your quilt.

It is important to quilt the thread painting to the other quilt layers to prevent buckling. Sky or background areas that were left untouched can be quilted or stippled, adding more interest to the thread painting and holding it to the backing. If no additional visual stitching is required, trace along the basic shapes in the thread painting using monofilament thread so that the stitches disappear, but serve their purpose. Use clear thread for the light areas and smoke for the dark areas. Bobbin thread should match the backing fabric.

Binding

After quilting is complete, trim the batting and backing even with the quilt top.

Binding a project usually requires a strip of fabric, 2¼" to 2½", cut from selvage to selvage. A wider strip can be used on a quilt with a thicker batting, or for a wider binding edge.

Fold the binding strip in half lengthwise with wrong sides together and press.

Match the binding raw edges to the quilt raw edges. Using a walking foot and a ¼" seam allowance, sew the binding in place on opposite quilt sides.

Fold the folded edge of the binding to the quilt back, covering the previous stitching line. Pin in place before sewing on the final two strips. When attaching the remaining binding strips, fold under the beginning and end of the strip to line up with the first binding strip fold, creating a nice clean square corner.

To sew the binding in place by machine, pin it in the ditch of the seam from the quilt front, making sure that the pins catch the binding on the back. Stitch in the ditch of the seam from the front, pulling out the pins as you go.

If you prefer, hand stitch the binding in place.

Unbound Finishing

If you prefer not to bind your quilt, consider using what I call the "pillowcase" method for finishing.

After assembling the quilt top, but before adding any additional quilting, place the quilt back and front right sides together with a layer of batting underneath the quilt back. Stitch around the edges of the quilt top using a ¼" seam allowance, leaving a 6" to 8" opening for turning.

Trim the corners to reduce bulk. Turn the quilt right-side out and hand stitch the opening closed. Lightly press the edges.

Quilt the layers together using monofilament thread.

Thread painting and thread sketching can add an exciting element to many of the things you already make. I hope that you will try the projects in this book, but that you will also adapt the technique and make it your own. When people admire your finished work and ask "how did you do that?!" you don't need to share with them just how easy it was.

Projects

African Pillow

Finished size: 24" x 7" (or customize to fit the cloth)
Technique: Thread painting
Special focus: Non-standard size pillows, embellishments
Skill level: Starter

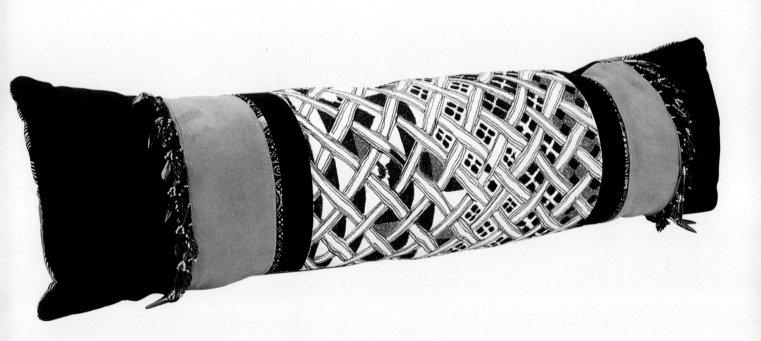

Kuba cloth is woven raffia with tufted embroidery made by the Kuba people of Africa. The artform is an ancient one, and characteristically Kuba cloth is based on geometric designs, but beautifully asymmetrical. Each piece of Kuba cloth is made by hand and takes a month or more to create. They are not only all unique, but bold and striking. This thread painting is based on a Kuba cloth in my own collection. The free-flowing design looks quite modern to me. You can make the pillow any size or shape that suits your needs, with either a ready-made insert, or a stuffed custom size like this one.

Materials (For the featured pillow; alter as needed for other sizes.)

Kuba Cloth

1 sheet computer printable fabric, 8½" x 11"

¼ yd. black cotton fabric, 45" wide, for borders

¾"-wide strip ethnic print, 45" wide, for flange

¼ yd. beige faux suede, 45" wide, for borders

¼ yd. print fabric, 45" wide, for backing

Lightweight batting

Tools and Notions

½ yd. beaded trim

Embroidery hoop

Thread

Darning foot

Polyester stuffing

Zipper foot

Cutting

Black fabric:

    2 rectangles, 1½" x 7½"

    2 rectangles, 4½" x 7½"

Print fabric:

    2 rectangles, 7½" x ¾"

Beige faux suede:

    2 rectangles, 2½" x 7½"

Backing fabric:

    1 strip, 7½" x 24½"

Batting:

    2 strips, 7½" x 24½"

Construction

Note: All seam allowances are ¼".

1. Scan Kuba cloth design and print on the inkjet-printable fabric. Remove the paper backing. Center the printed sheet on batting the size of the finished pillow. Hoop the fabric and thread paint the design, re-hooping as needed. Don't worry about following the printed lines exactly — the beauty of Kuba Cloth is its irregularity. Trim the thread painted piece (not the batting layer) to 7½" x 10½".

2. Return the machine to normal stitch settings. Stitching through the batting, join the narrow black bands to each 7½" side of the thread painted section.

3. To attach the printed flange, fold the strip in half wrong sides together and press. Stitch it to the outside edges of each black strip, matching the raw edges and trimming the length to match the bands. Join the faux suede bands.

4. To attach the beaded trim, pin it to the raw edge of the faux suede band only, without the batting. Sew it in place using a zipper foot to get as close to the beaded edge as possible.

5. Turn this edge of the fabric band under, making sure that the beading header is not visible.

6. Place the wide black border strip so that it sits on the batting and underlaps the beaded border by ¼". Pin in place. Using a zipper foot and clear thread, sew long the edge as close to the beads as possible.

7. Trim the pillow to its final size and layer with batting. (The use of batting under the front and back of the pillow will ensure that the stuffing doesn't look lumpy.)

8. Place the pillow front and back, right sides together, and stitch around the edges, leaving a small opening on one side for turning. Trim away any beads in the seam allowance, and tuck the remainder into the pillow while sewing to avoid breaking a needle.

9. Stuff the pillow to the desired fullness. An 18" ruler is great for pushing the stuffing into this long narrow pillow.

10. Hand stitch the opening closed.

Baby Bib

Technique: Thread sketching
Special focus: Double thread; filling in areas
Skill level: Starter

What a beautiful handmade gift for a new baby — and so easy, just a simple thread sketch and binding! Choose the featured teddy bear and heart motif, any of the designs from the baby quilt, or use a design of your own.

Materials

¼ yd. white cotton fabric, 45" wide,
   for bib front and back
Lightweight batting

Tools and Notions

Freezer paper

Tear-away stabilizer

Double-fold bias tape

Thread

Topstitch needle

Darning foot

Stiletto

Embroidery hoop

Cutting

2 rectangles white cotton, 9" x 13"
1 rectangle batting, 9" x 13".

Construction

1. Print the motif onto the tear-away stabilizer.

2. Trace the bib pattern from the pattern pages in the back of the book onto the freezer paper.

3. Layer the white cotton rectangles on each side of the batting and pin the printed stabilizer on top, centering the motif.

4. Wind two bobbins with the same color thread and place them on the spool pin with both threads feeding off the back. Thread the needle with the double threads. Wind a white bobbin and insert it into the machine. Set the machine for free-motion stitching; lower the feed dogs and install the darning foot.

5. Test-stitch on a sample and adjust the tension as needed. A high number setting is usually required when using multiple threads. Follow the directions for sketching with multiple threads on page 22.

6. Outline the design and trim the jump stitches.

7. Remove the tear-away stabilizer.

8. Fill in the design details — the eyes, nose and widen the heart outline. (Hooping sometimes helps here.)

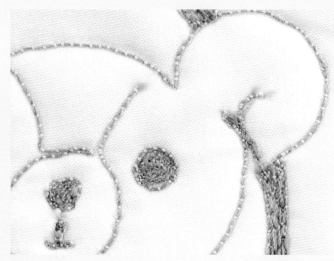

9. Lightly press the freezer paper bib pattern onto the stitched fabric, lining up the design placement with your stitched design. Cut the bib around the pattern edge and remove the paper.

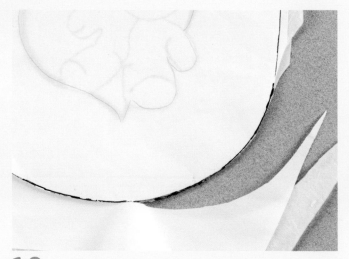

10. Raise the feed dogs and return the machine to normal stitch settings. Baste the cut edges together ⅛" from the edge.

11. Reset the tension and machine settings for normal sewing. Change the bobbin and top thread to match the bias tape.

12. Bind the upper bib edge. Use the needle-down function, if your machine has it, to help hold the bias in place as you stitch; reposition the bias and tuck in the batting using a stiletto if needed. Trim the binding even with the bib edges.

13. Bind the bib outer edges, extending and sewing 8" at the beginning and end for the neck ties. Trim the binding ends diagonally and use a few stitches to help prevent raveling.

Bias binding is not folded exactly in the middle, there is one side that is slightly shorter than the other. The short side should be on the top as you sew, insuring that the back will be caught in your stitching.

Baby Quilt

Finished size: 41" square
Technique: Thread sketching
Special focus: Double thread
Skill level: Starter

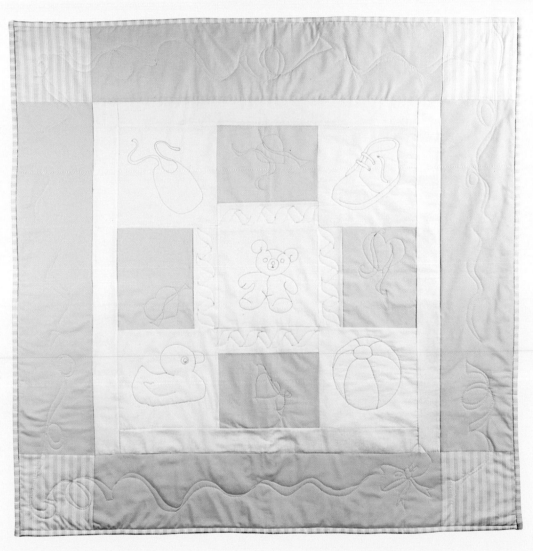

Simple pastel colors and large thread-sketched blocks make this quilt a quick, but impressive baby gift. Accent the solid colors with stripes for even more pizzazz. Use the simple line drawings provided, or find your own in coloring books, children's books or take inspiration from other fabrics used in the baby's room. Before the quilt is layered, you can add the baby's name and birth date on the border using the instructions in the lettering section of the book.

Materials

¼ yd. white fabric, 45" wide, for blocks

1 yd. blue fabric, 45" wide, for blocks and outer borders

½ yd. yellow fabric, 45" wide, for blocks and inner borders

½ yd. striped fabric, 45" wide, for binding and corner blocks

1½ yd. fabric, 45" wide, for backing

Lightweight batting

Tools and Notions

Tear-away stabilizer

Thread

Topstitch needle

Darning foot

Cutting

White fabric:

   5 squares, 8½"

Blue fabric:

   4 strips, 6½" x width of fabric

   4 strips, 6½" x 8½"

Yellow fabric:

   5 strips, 2½" x width of fabric

Striped fabric:

   4 strips, 2½" x width of fabric

   4 squares, 6½"

Construction

Note: All seam allowances are ¼". Directions are given for using multiple threads, but, you can use a single thread.

1. Wind two bobbins of blue thread for sketching and one of white thread for the bobbin. Place the two blue bobbins on the spool pin feeding off the back; thread the needle with both threads. Insert the white bobbin into the machine. Set the machine for free-motion stitching; lower the feed dogs and install the darning foot. (Follow the directions for using multiple threads on page 22.)

2. Print the block designs onto tear-away stabilizer,

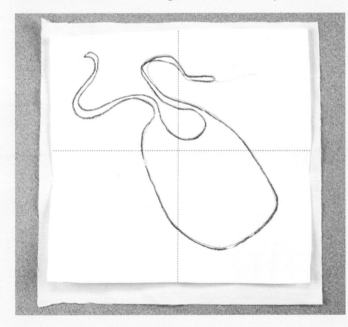

3. Fold each white square in half, and then in half again; lightly press to establish the center points. Line up the creases with the dotted lines on the patterns and pin in place. The dotted lines are for placement only and do not get sketched.

4. Test-stitch on scraps of fabric and batting to adjust the tension.

5. Hoop each white block with the tear-away stabilizer pattern on top. Sketch all the designs, cut the jump threads and remove the stabilizer. For any areas that will need to be filled-in (like the teddy's eyes) sketch the outline, remove the paper and then fill these areas with thread.

6. Return the machine to normal stitch settings. Join one yellow strip to the long side of each blue rectangle and trim the ends evenly. Press the seams to one side.

7. Stitch the quilt center blocks together as shown in photograph.

8. Stitch yellow strips along the upper and lower edges of the quilt center, trimming the ends to match the piecing. Repeat for the sides.

9. Square up the quilt and then stitch the blue borders to the quilt upper and lower edges.

10. Trim the remaining blue strips to match the length of the quilt center, plus ½". Stitch a striped square to each end of the strips, making sure the stripes on the corner blocks go in the same direction.

11. Attach the remaining outer borders, aligning the corner square seams with the yellow border seamlines.

12. Layer the backing, batting and pieced quilt top. Pin all the edges together being sure the quilt top and backing are completely flat.

13. Quilt on the lines of the thread sketched designs with blue or clear thread so that they will be seen on the back and also create a trapunto effect on the front.

14. Bind the quilt edges to finish.

Butterfly Quilt

Finished size: 30" x 32"
Technique: Thread painting
Special focus: Thread painting from a photo, specialty threads
Skill level: Comfortable

Butterfly motifs are popular with quilters, and for good reason — they are delicate and colorful. I used actual photos of butterflies as a starting point for the featured quilt. The stitched butterflies are an extension of my imagination. Their colors and designs may not be true to nature, but they satisfy my artistic vision. Coupled with complementary batik fabrics, the resulting quilt brings to mind spring days watching butterflies flutter from flower to flower.

Materials

5 sheets of inkjet-printable fabric, 8½" x 11"

½ yd. batik fabric, 45" wide, for outer borders

½ yd. fabric, 45" wide, for sashing

½ yd. fabric, 45" wide, for accent blocks.

Note: Assorted color scraps may be used instead of a single color, as shown in the featured quilt.

1 yd. fabric, 45" wide, for backing

Lightweight batting

Tools and Notions

Tear-away stabilizer

Threads

Darning foot

Press cloth

Appliqué scissors (optional)

Butterfly designs

Cutting

Sashing fabric:

   16 rectangles, 5" x 3½"

Accent fabric:

   16 blocks, 3½" square.

Batik fabric:

   4 strips, 3½" x width of fabric

Construction

Note: All seam allowances are ¼".

1. Scan and print the butterfly designs shown on page 131 onto inkjet-printable fabric.

Print two per page, leaving enough area around each image to cut 5" square blocks. Use the extra space to print quilt labels. Remove the paper backing from the printed fabrics.

2. Cut the printed squares apart and layer each onto a batting scrap. The batting does not need to extend to the block edges, as it will be trimmed away after thread painting, leaving a trapunto effect.

3. Back each square with tear-away stabilizer. Set the machine for free-motion stitching; lower the feed dogs and install the darning foot. Thread paint each butterfly. Enjoy the process and be creative — this isn't a time to worry about being true to nature, have fun with color and with special threads like metallic and glitter. Many of the butterflies have small areas that will require jump stitches between them. Stitch these first so the background color (like black) can go right over the jump threads and you won't need to trim them. When using metallic or glitter threads, fill the area in first with a thread color, use a very small amount of the metallic or glitter thread over the top as an accent. Tear away any paper that isn't stitched on. (Not all the paper will be removable.)

4. Lightly press the butterflies from the top using a press cloth to protect the threads.

5. Using the butterfly outline as a guide, carefully trim away the batting outside the stitched area. Appliqué scissors are great for this, as one side is blunt, to help prevent snipping into the fabric.

6. Trim the butterfly blocks, allowing at least ½" above and below the image. Each row needs three butterfly blocks the same size, so plan the layout and trim accordingly.

7. Determine the placement of the accent blocks.

8. Return the machine to normal stitch settings. Stitch a sashing strip to the right side of each butterfly block and to the left of those on the left hand side of the quilt. Trim even with the butterfly blocks. Use the finished quilt photo as a guide.

9. One row at a time, sew together the sashing strips and accent squares, trimming as needed.

10. Join the sashing/square rows to the butterfly rows, alternating until the quilt top is complete. Follow the photograph for details.

11. Stitch the outer border to the upper and lower edges of the quilt. Repeat for the sides.

12. With right sides together, layer the quilt top and backing with the batting under the back. Pin all the edges together; trim the batting and backing to match the quilt top edges. Stitch ¼" from the outer edge around the quilt, leaving at least 6" opening for turning. Trim the corners to reduce bulk.

13. Turn the quilt right-side out, gently poking out the corners. Lightly press the edges and hand stitch the opening closed.

14. Using monofilament thread, quilt around the butterflies and in the ditch of all the seams, or quilt as desired. Sew on the binding.

Butterflies Meet Technology!

I created the butterfly blocks using Photoshop. Check your owner's manual for instructions for your software program.

1. Choose **New** from the **File** menu and create a 5" by 5" image. Click the foreground color in the toolbox and choose a pale background color from the Adobe Color Picker dialog box that appears.

2. From the **Filters** menu, choose **Texture** > **Texturizer**, and select **Sandstone** from the options that appear. Click OK to apply this filter to the background image.

3. From the **Filters** menu, choose **Brush Strokes** > **Crosshatch**, and click OK to apply.

4. Choose **File** > **Save** to save the image as "Butterfly Background" so you can use it to complete each butterfly design.

1. Choose **File** > **Open** and select a butterfly photograph.

2. Use the Crop tool to eliminate most of the original background.

3. Choose **Image** > **Image Size** to set the image width to 5". Keep the image height proportional to avoid any image distortion.

4. If you closed the "Butterfly Background" image, choose **File** > **Open** to open the background image.

5. Copy and paste the butterfly to the background square.

6. Use the Magic Wand tool to select the background color of the original butterfly photo and delete it. You should be able to see the new background you created behind the butterfly. Use the erase tool to clean up any leftover background.

7. Choose **File** > **Save** and rename the completed block. Save the file as a JPEG image.

Dog Quilt

Finished size: Approximately 30" square
Technique: Thread painting
Special focus: Scanning images for thread painting
Skill level: Comfortable

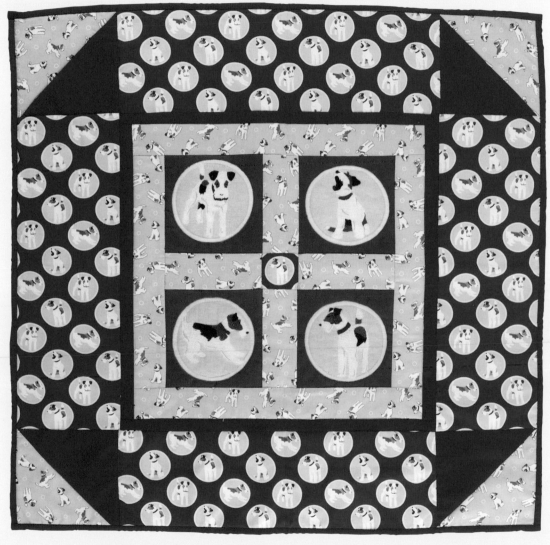

Sometimes you find a fabric that you just have to buy — that was the case with these two cute coordinating dog fabrics. As much as I loved the dogs, they were too small to thread paint, and I wanted them to be the focal point of my quilt. I scanned and enlarged the images to thread paint, so the feature blocks coordinate with the original fabric print. Your final quilt will undoubtedly be different from the one shown here, but these instructions will give you an idea about how to proceed with your own fabric choice.

Materials

1 yd. fabric with image(s) appropriate for scanning and
    thread painting, 45" wide

½ yd. each of one or two complementary fabrics,
    45" wide

2 sheets inkjet-printable fabric, 8½" x 11"

Lightweight batting

Tools and Notions

Tear-away stabilizer

Thread

Darning foot

Preparation

Note: These general directions apply to any quilt pattern you prefer.

1. Identify the section or sections of commercially printed fabric that you want to feature. Scan the fabric at a 200 to 300dpi setting, or the weave of the fabric will show.

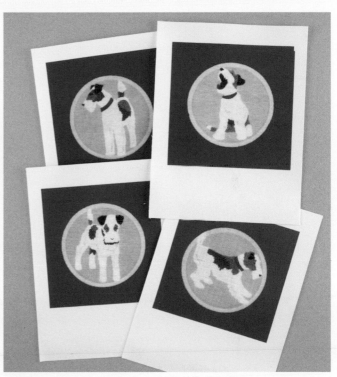

2. Use a graphics program to clean up the image if needed. In the case of the dogs, I brought up the contrast, lightened the image, and actually filled in the red areas so that they had no hint of the original fabric weave showing. Adjust colors as needed to coordinate with the complementary fabrics.

3. Print the image(s) on the inkjet-printable fabric; remove the backing.

Construction

1. Layer the printed images over thin batting backed with tear-away stabilizer or use a hoop.

2. Set the machine for free-motion stitching; lower the feed dogs and install the darning foot. Thread-paint the images.

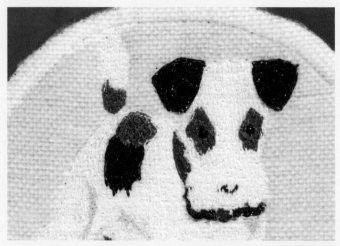

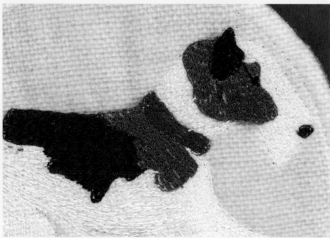

3. Remove the stabilizer and trim the jump threads.

4. Trim the blocks to the desired size, depending on your selected quilt pattern.

5. Complete the quilt top. For this one, I chose to keep the design simple and break up the two fabrics with red.

6. Use a walking foot to attach the batting-backed sections to the other parts of the quilt. Because the batting is thin, there is no problem in layering another piece of batting under the entire quilt, leaving the thread painted areas with a double layer of batting. With clear thread, quilt in these sections to prevent puckering.

Dragonfly Tote Bag

Finished size: 12" x 14"
Technique: Thread sketching
Special focus: Metallic and glitter threads
Skill level: Comfortable

For a day on the town or a picnic in the park, this Japanese inspired tote bag is just the thing to carry your essentials. The use of metallic and glitter threads gives sparkle to the dragonfly wings, just the way real ones catch the sunlight. Start with the basic shape provided and add your personal touches to the wing detail. Like all the other projects in this book, use this as a starting point to express your personal style – use any image you like and vary the fabrics for a totally different look.

71

Materials

½ yd. solid-color fabric, 45" wide, for image background, bottom and straps

¾ yd. coordinating fabric, 45" wide, for back and borders

½ yd. cotton fabric, 45" wide, for lining

Lightweight batting

Tools and Notions

Thread

Tear-away stabilizer

Metallic needle

Darning foot

Walking foot

Cutting

Background fabric:

    1 rectangle, 8½" x 6½", for dragonfly block

    2 strips 4" x width of fabric, for straps

    From one strip cut:

    1 rectangle, 4" x 14½", for tote bottom.

Coordinating fabric:

    1 rectangle, 14½" x 12½"

    2 strips, 3½" x width of fabric

Lining fabric:

    2 squares, 14½"

Construction
Note: All seam allowances are ¼".

1. Stitch a coordinating fabric strip to frame the upper, lower and sides of the solid-color rectangle.

2. Stitch the solid-color tote bottom to the lower edge of the framed section, and then add the back to the opposite side of the bottom.

3. Press the seams in one direction and back with batting; pin the edges in place.

4. Print the dragonfly pattern onto tear-away stabilizer and position it on the framed block. The dragonfly may be straight or at an angle. Remember, it needs to be positioned so that the tail points towards the seam between the squares.

5. Adjust the machine for free-motion stitching, install the darning foot and lower the feed dogs. Using a metallic needle, test-stitch on scraps to perfect the stitch tension using metallic thread. Thread sketch the outline of the dragonfly and remove the stabilizer.

6. Fill in the lines and details in the dragonfly wings. There is no right or wrong way, just have fun with it. Stitch as much, or as little, as you like. Use the picture in this sample as a guide, or look at other pictures of dragonflies and put the lines where you want them. Glitter thread is a good choice here. It will add iridescent sparkle to the interior wings.

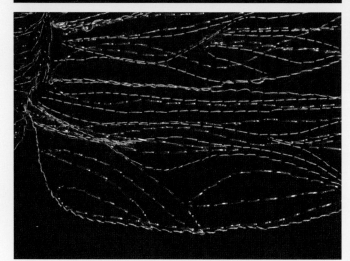

7. When stitching is complete, trim the batting to match the fabric layer.

8. Return the machine to normal stitch settings.

9. Determine the desired length of the tote straps (usually around 30") and trim the solid-color fabric strips to this length, plus ½" for seams.

10. Fold each strap in half lengthwise with wrong sides together and press.

11. Fold each of the two folded edges in to line up with the center fold, and press again. Fold in half again creating a 1"-wide strap.

12. Edgestitch both straps along the folded edges with matching or clear thread.

13. Fold the tote bag in half, right sides together, lining up the seams from the bottom strip. Sew the two side seams using a ¼" seam allowance.

14. Pin the straps to the front and back of the tote bag, using the edge of the interior rectangle to line up their placement. Make sure they do not get twisted. Gather up the straps and pin them to the body of the tote to keep them out of the way.

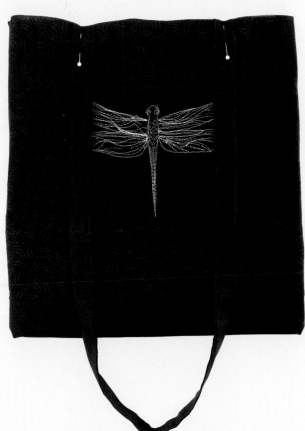

15. Place the two pieces of interior fabric with right sides together. Sew the side seams using a ¼" seam allowance.

19. Tuck the lining into the tote bag and press the upper edge.

20. Turn the tote bag inside out and push the corners into the lining corners. Fold all layers together so the lining seam is in the center, forming a point. Measure down 2" from the point and sew across.

16. With right sides together, slide the tote bag into the lining, matching side seams and upper edges. Keep the strap out of the way.

17. Stitch the lining to the tote around the upper edge using a walking foot.

18. Pull the lining out of the bag and press under ½" on each of the raw edges; edgestitch the folds together.

21. Push the lining back into the tote.

Evening Purse —Two Ways

Finished size: 6" x 10"
Technique: Thread painting
Special focus: thread painted
    image or thread painting a
    fabric
Skill level: Comfortable

This adorable evening purse can be made two ways — with a fabric you like filled in with thread, or with a computer-printed image. Either way, you'll have a unique and lovely purse for a night on the town. Use a costume jewelry chain like the one used here as a strap, or leave off the strap for a clever clutch. Buttons or beads sewn to the front hold the top closed, or create a button-and-loop closure.

Materials

Inkjet-printable fabric sheet, 8½" x 11" or ½ yd. fabric print, 45" wide

¼ yd. fabric, 45" wide, for borders (computer printed version only)

½ yd. cotton fabric, 45" wide, for lining

Lightweight batting

Tools and Notions

Thread

Old costume jewelry necklace, or double-fold bias tape, for strap

Beads or button for closure

¼ yd. beaded trim (optional)

Seam sealant (optional)

Tear-away stabilizer

Freezer paper

Darning foot

Walking foot (optional)

Evening bag pattern

Construction
Note: All seam allowances are ¼".

Starting with a Thread Painting

1. Choose an image. Keep in mind that half will be the front and half the back.

2. Print onto computer printable fabric. Remove the paper.

3. Add one or more borders equaling 2" on each side and lower edge of the printed piece. Add a 4" border at the top. This will be the front flap of the purse.

Starting with a fabric

Identify the area of the fabric to be used for the evening purse. Instructions are the same from this point.

1. Trace the purse pattern onto freezer paper, and lightly press it, shiny side down, onto the fabric.

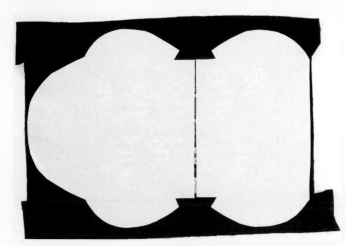

2. For commercially printed fabric, position the template on the fabric print, centering large motifs, if applicable.

3. Cut out around the shape and remove the freezer paper

4. Layer each piece onto a thin batting, pinning a piece of tear-away paper to the back for stabilization (or use a hoop).

5. Set the machine for free-motion stitching; lower the feed dogs and install the darning foot.

6. Thread-paint as much as you want. Remove any stabilizer that can be removed. Trim all the jump threads.

7. Add any beads or surface embellishing before constructing.

8. Return the sewing machine to its normal settings.

9. With right sides together and using a walking foot, stitch the bag side seams with a ¼" seam allowance, from the lower corner notch to the upper edge.

10. Sew along the bottom edge. If you want beads to hang from the bottom, attach them while sewing this seam.

11. Bring together the raw edges of the notch and sew across, forming the purse bottom.

12. Cut out the lining using the same freezer paper template that you used for the purse.

13. Stitch the lining side seams, but leave the bottom open.

14. With right sides together, pin the top of the lining to the top of the purse. Line up the side seams and sew them together.

15. Turn under the seam allowances at the lower lining edge and topstitch. Push the lining into the purse.

16. Add any buttons, beads or other closures.

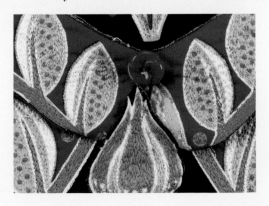

17. Hand stitch the strap to the bag.

Bias Braid

To create a strap using double-fold bias tape, pin one end of three equal lengths to an ironing board.

The finished strap length depends on your preference. Keep in mind that some of the bias length will be taken up in the braiding process.

Braid the bias strands and press. Stitch across each end, fold them under, and attach to the purse.

Japanese Ladies Pillow

Finished size: 14" square
Technique: Thread painting
Special focus: Thread painting a fabric
Skill level: Comfortable

With so many beautiful fabrics available, it is easy to find one to use as a focal point for a lovely thread-painted pillow. What a great way to make a pillow unique, just by using a fabric design. Choose a fabric with a "panel" or simply identify an area for a wonderful pillow center.

Materials

Focus fabric for center panel, yardage will vary depending on the fabric print; the featured pillow required ½ yd.

¼ yd. of one or two coordinating fabrics, 45" wide, for borders

¼ yd. fabric, 45" wide, for pillow back

Lightweight batting

Tools and Notions

Tear-away stabilizer

14" square pillow form

Polyester fiberfill (optional)

Thread

Darning foot

Cutting

Focus fabric:

Identify the fabric area that appeals to you as the focal point of the design. The size and shape of the area doesn't matter, as borders will be added to make it a finished 14" square. Cut the area out of the fabric, allowing ½" extra around the edges for seam allowances

Backing fabric:

2 pieces, 9" x 14½"

Batting:

15" square

Construction
Note: All seam allowances are ¼".

1. Center the focus fabric over the batting and back with a piece of tear-away stabilizer. Pin in place outside of the design area.

2. Set up the machine for free-motion stitching; lower the feed dogs and install the darning foot.

3. Thread paint the designated design. Remember, not all areas need to be thread painted for dramatic effect. Re-evaluate periodically to decide how much stitching is needed.

4. Tear away the stabilizer and clip all jump threads on both sides of the work.

5. Return the sewing machine to normal stitch settings.

6. Add borders as desired. If distracting elements from the fabric design are showing (like partial sections of neighboring print motifs), cover them with shaped border pieces.

7. Trim the finished pillow front to 14½" square.

8. To create the pillow back, turn the long edge of each 9" x 14½" piece under ¼" and press. Turn under ¼" again and topstitch the folded edges in place.

9. Overlap the pillow back hemmed edges to form a 14½" square.

10. Match the pillow back and front edges with right sides together. Sew the perimeter seam. Trim the corners to reduce bulk.

11. Turn the pillow right-side out and insert the pillow form. Add a little batting into the corners to make them look pretty.

Nature's Kaleidoscope

Finished size: 33" x 37"
Technique: Thread painting
Special focus: Images larger than 8½" x 11"
Skill level: Confident

I started with a pretty pink flower photo, but wanted to create something more unusual, more artistic and more spectacular — and a thread painting larger than 8½" x 11". This wall hanging is the result of printing the image four times (twice in mirror image) and combining them to create a kaleidoscope. Try it with your own photos, and turn pretty into pretty amazing!

Materials

4 inkjet-printable fabric sheets, 8½" x 11"

¼ yd. each of three fabrics, 45" wide, for the inside* borders

¾ yd. fabric, 45" wide, for the outside border

1 yd. backing fabric, 45" wide

Lightweight batting

*Yardage is based on quilt shown

Tool and Notions

Tear-away stabilizer

Thread

Darning foot

Cutting

First inner border fabric:
   Strips, 1¼" x width of fabric

Second inner border fabric:
   Strips, 1¾" strips x width of fabric

Third inner border fabric:
   Strips, 2" x width of fabric

Outer border fabric:
   Strips, 6½" x width of fabric.

Construction
Note: All seam allowances are ¼".

1. Select an image and print two copies and two in mirror image on paper to "audition" them for the kaleidoscope arrangement. (Look in your programs and/or printer properties for a "flip" or "mirror image" setting.) When you're satisfied with the arrangement, print the images onto the inkjet-printable fabric sheets. Remove the paper backing.

Remember to allow margins on the printed page for seam allowances.

2. Carefully line up the image match points and seam two fabric pieces together. Press the seam allowances open. Repeat for the other pair, and then join all four.

3. Layer the pieced image over batting and back with tear-away stabilizer. (Four pieces taped together will work best.)

4. Set the machine for free-motion stitching; lower the feed dogs and install the darning foot.

5. Begin thread painting in the center and work out. As you work on each section, complete the other three like areas at the same time so that they look similar. Glitter threads work well as accents.

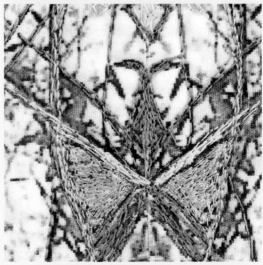

6. When the thread painting is complete, square up the edges, tear away the stabilizer, trim the jump threads on both sides of the work and square off.

7. Return the machine to normal stitch settings. Stitch the first inner border to the kaleidoscope. Repeat for each additional inner border. Press seams toward the border.

8. Stitch the outer border strips to the inner border in the same manner.

9. Layer the quilt top and backing with right sides together. Lay the batting on the wrong side of the backing fabric. Using a walking foot, sew around the edges leaving a 6" opening for turning.

10. Trim the corners to reduce bulk and turn the quilt right-side out. Hand stitch the opening closed.

11. Stitch in the ditch of the seams and quilt the thread-painted area. Use monofilament thread for invisible stitching.

Passport or iPod Case

Finished size: 4½" square
Technique: Thread sketching
Special focus: Lettering
Skill level: Starter

Use this handy little case when you travel to hold your passport and boarding passes so you can get to them whenever they are needed. Not traveling? It makes a great carrying case for an iPod or even your eyeglasses! This is a good project for using leftover pieces of fabric from other projects. Replace the Chinese character for "joy" with your own initial, if you prefer.

Materials

Small scrap of light-color fabric, approximately 2½" square

¼ yd. coordinating fabric, 45" wide, for borders

¼ yd. cotton fabric, 45" wide, for lining

Lightweight batting

Tools and Notions

1 yd. double-fold bias tape, for strap

Tear-away stabilizer

Thread

Darning foot

Cutting

Coordinating fabric:

   1 square, 5"

   1 strip, 1¾" x width of fabric

Lining fabric:

   1 rectangle, 10" x 5".

Construction

Note: All seam allowances are ¼".

1. Stitch a 1¾" strip to each side of the 2½" center square and trim the lengths evenly. Repeat for the upper and lower edges, pressing all seam allowances toward the sewn strips.

2. Stitch the 5" square of coordinating fabric to one edge of the pieced front.

3. Pin the pieced fabric to the batting and trim the batting even with the fabric.

4. Print the Chinese character or initial onto tear-away stabilizer. Center the printed stabilizer over the solid fabric square and pin in place outside the design area.

5. Adjust the machine for free-motion stitching; lower the feed dogs and install a darning foot.

6. Stitch around the outline and carefully remove the stabilizer.

7. Fill in the outline with thread. Trim the jump threads on both sides of the work.

8. Return the machine to normal stitch settings. Sew the lining to the case at both short edges and then turn the case right-side out

9. Using matching or clear thread, sew the bias tape closed along the open edge.

10. Pin the bias strap to both sides of the case front within the seam allowance (avoid twisting). Fold under the raw ends of the bias to finish.

11. Fold the case in half, right sides together, and stitch the side seams, catching the bias as you stitch.

12. Finish the raw edges with a zigzag stitch.

Table Runner With Leaves

Finished size: 4½" square
Technique: Thread sketching
Special focus: Thread-painted embroidery
Skill level: Comfortable

My favorite season is autumn — the colors of the leaves and trees are so lovely I chose to capture them forever in thread. Background batik fabric provides texture and interest without a competing pattern. The leaves are scans of real leaves from my yard. Scan your own or use the ones provided in the back of the book, and have fun coloring them with thread. For a fun variation, cut leaves out of a leaf print fabric.

Materials

¼ yd. each of two light-value fabrics, 45" wide, for blocks

⅜ yd. contrasting fabric, 45" wide, for borders and sashing

½ yd. fabric, 45" wide, for backing

⅛ yd. fabric, 45" wide for flange

Lightweight batting

Inkjet-printable fabric

Tools and Notions

Paper-backed fusible web

Thread

Darning foot

Cutting

Light fabric:

   From each light fabric, 6 squares, 5"

Border fabric:

   3 strips, 3½" x width of fabric

Flange fabric:

   3 strips, 1" x width of fabric.

Construction

Note: All seam allowances are ¼".

1. Stitch four blocks together, alternating colors; repeat to make three sets.

2. Sew a sashing strip between each four-patch unit, being sure to keep the block colors in the same order.

3. Fold and press the flange strips in half lengthwise, wrong sides together.

4. Pin the raw edges to the pieced runner on the long sides. Stitch in place, and repeat for the short ends.

5. Sew the borders to the two short ends and press open. Add the border strips to the long sides.

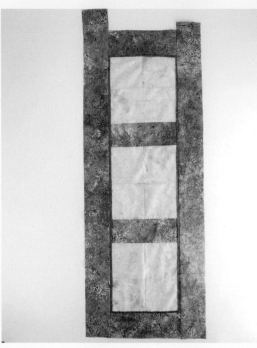

9. Position the leaves on the quilt top as desired. Fuse the leaves in place, following the manufacturer's instructions.

If you have seams that don't quite line up, it is a great place to put a leaf.

6. Layer the pieced runner onto batting and trim the batting to size.

7. Print the leaves onto inkjet-printable fabric. Rough-cut the images or cut leaves out of commercial fabric.

10. Set the machine for free-motion stitching; lower the feed dogs and install the darning foot.

11. Thread paint the leaves, extending the stitching just beyond the cut edges.

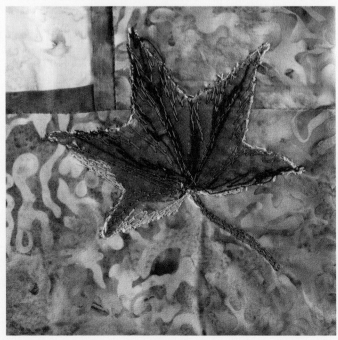

8. Following the manufacturer's instructions, back the leaves with paper-backed fusible web. Trim the leaves closely along their outlines. Since stems are so thin and tricky to fuse, I often cut them off and re-create them in thread.

12. Press the quilt lightly when stitching is complete and block if necessary.

13. Return the machine to the normal sewing settings.

14. Place the backing and quilt top with right sides together. Using a walking foot, stitch the quilt top to the backing leaving a 6" to 8" opening for turning.

15. Trim the corners to reduce bulk and turn the quilt right-side out. Hand stitch the opening closed.

16. Using monofilament thread, quilt around the leaves and in the ditch of the borders and sashings.

Teatime Redwork Quilt

Finished size: 34" x 42"
Technique: Thread sketching
Special focus: Rayon or trilobal thread
Skill level: Comfortable

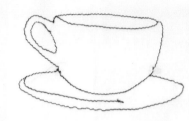

Dual Duty Plus Thread   *Rayon Thread*   *Trilobal Rayon Thread*

Redwork, popular in the 1940s, was traditionally done by hand. As soon as I saw this fabric, I knew I had to use the adorable children drinking tea for my own Redwork quilt, but done the faster, easier way with thread sketching. Any red and white fabric will work with these figures, but, if you don't like red, think about bluework or black-work — any single-color stitching works. I used trilobal rayon thread for this project, but any thread is appropriate

Materials

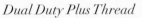

½ yd. white or off white fabric, 45" wide, for Redwork blocks

½ yd. red print fabric, 45" wide, for sashing*

¼ yd. red solid fabric, 45" wide, for blocks

½ yd. striped fabric, 45" wide, for outside border

1 yd. backing fabric, 45" wide

Lightweight batting

The focus fabric used here is "Everything but the Kitchen Sink," by RJR Fabrics.

Tools and Notions

Tear-away stabilizer

Thread

Darning foot

Cutting

White fabric:

   12 blocks, 6"

Sashing fabric:

   4 strips, 4" x width of fabric

Solid red:

   20 squares, 4"

Striped fabric:

   4 strips, 3" x width of fabric

For a smaller quilt, use 4, 6 or 9 Redwork blocks.

Construction

Note: All seam allowances are ¼".

1. Print the Redwork designs onto tear-away stabilizer and pin each one to a white square, centering the design.

2. Set the machine for free-motion stitching; lower the feed dogs and install the darning foot.

3. Thread sketch the designs and carefully tear away the stabilizer. Hold your fingers on the stitching line while removing the stabilizer to avoid pulling out the line of stitching.

4. Trim all the stitched blocks to 5½" square, centering the designs.

5. Return the machine to normal stitch settings.

6. Stitch sashing between the blocks and trim the length to match the blocks.

7. Stitch alternating solid red and print blocks together, following the photograph.

8. Alternating rows of pieced blocks and thread-sketched/sashing blocks, stitch the rows together to form the quilt center, matching adjacent seamlines. Press the seam allowances to one side.

9. Stitch the borders to the outside quilt edges.

10. Layer the quilt top, right sides together, with the backing and batting. Using a walking foot, sew around the edge leaving a 6" opening for turning.

11. Trim the corners to reduce bulk and turn the quilt right-side out.

12. Stitch in the ditch of the seams to quilt.

Thread Sketched Shirt

Finished size: Custom
Technique: Thread sketching
Focus: Thread sketching small pieces
Skill level: Starter

Create a custom "art garment" that allows you to express your own creativity. Start with a plain shirt and arrange designs to thread sketch. Use geometric shapes like those provided, or find shapes and designs of your own. Try different thread colors or a different colored shirt and put as many, or as few, designs on as you like — you are the designer.

103

Materials

Solid-color shirt, cotton or linen

Tools and Notions

Tear-away stabilizer

Thread

Darning foot

Construction

1. Print the designs shown in the back of the book onto tear-away stabilizer. Rough-cut each one and pin onto the shirt front and back.

2. Try on the shirt to be sure that no designs are centered at the bust point, or other unflattering area. Be sure you like the placement of the designs before you begin.

3. Back the area under each design with unprinted stabilizer to prevent puckering, or use a hoop.

4. Set the machine for free-motion stitching; lower the feed dogs and install the darning foot.

5. One motif at a time, stitch the outline of the shape and gently pull the stabilizer off the top only.

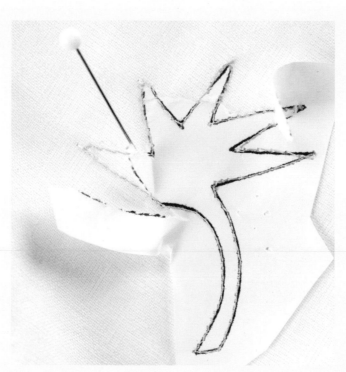

6. For a darker thread line, restitch any lines desired.

7. When the shirt designs are complete, remove the stabilizer from the underside and press.

Sketched Portrait From a Photo

Technique: Thread sketching
Special focus: Working from a photo
Skill level: Comfortable

This has always been one of my favorite photos of my two sons, taken when they were quite young. I decided that it would be a wonderful thread sketch, and a more dramatic way to display the photo. Obviously, I don't expect anyone who buys this book to want to make a thread sketch of my boys (as cute as I think they are!) but the instructions for this project are intended to give you the tools to turn your favorite photo into thread-sketched art.

Materials

Note: Materials will vary depending on the quilt design and the size chosen. All fabric amounts are for quilt shown.

Photo, back and white or color
½ yd. background fabric
½ yd. border fabric
1 yd. backing fabric
Thin batting

Tools and Notions

Wash-away stabilizer paper
Thread
Darning foot

Construction

1. When starting with a photograph, it is important to simplify the image to a line drawing. This can be done in several ways. If you have a scanner, the photograph can be scanned into the computer as a "black and white document." This setting is intended for black text on a white page, and therefore does not translate colors or even shades of grey. This is the way the portraits in this project were done.

2. Another way to change a photograph is in a program like Photoshop or Photoshop Elements. By using the "filters" in the pull-down menu, it is possible to "translate" the image so it is more easily read as a line drawing. If working from a color photo, start by changing it to black and white (image-mode-grayscale). The filters that work the best for this process are "artistic-poster edges" and "brushstrokes-ink outlines." Play with these and other filters until you get an image that would be easy to follow with a thread line.

3. Finally, if you have neither of the above options, print the image in black and white (as opposed to full color), and bring the lightness way up and the contrast way up. This should give you an image that you can follow with the thread lines.

4. If none of the above methods are available to you, take the photo to a commercial copy shop and ask for a copy (the size you want the final sketch to be) made light with high contrast — they may be able to print it right onto your stabilizer paper.

5. For this example, I blew up the image so that it was the size of two sheets of wash-away paper. I printed the two sheets with a little overlap of the images, so when I lined up the images, I was able to tape the two sheets of wash-away together for one large image.

6. I particularly like this technique when it is done in one color and complemented with the same color in the borders. It does not need to be black and white.

7. Remember that you are looking for artistic interpretation, not photographic realism. Leave some areas blank. Be creative and enjoy the process. It is amazing how few lines are truly needed to make a clear and identifiable image.

Colored thread can be just as effective as black.

8. Pin the printed stabilizer onto fabric with either regular or fusible batting underneath. Paper behind the batting may be helpful.

9. With feed dogs down and darning foot on the machine, follow the outlines.

10. Remove any large areas of paper and then soak it in water to remove any remaining paper. Sometimes a little gentle dish soap will help remove residual paper and an old toothbrush or a sea sponge can be used to gently scrub the paper out from heavily threaded areas.

11. Dry flat on a towel.

12. Square off and add borders — here I used only one border of a fabric that graduates from white to black and mitered it at the corners. Add one border, add several, make it whatever size you want.

13. Layer the finished quilt top onto batting and backing and quilt as you would any other quilt. I found that going over some of the sketch lines with the same color thread both deepened the color of the sketch, and gave more dimension to the final quilt. It is important to do some quilting in the sketch area.

Zach's Tree

Finished size: 21" x 22½"
Technique: Thread painting
Special focus: Thread painting from artwork
Skill level: Confident

My friend Zachary Ehrenreich is a very talented painter. One day, while at his house, I noticed a beautiful pastel sketch of a tree, and it was perfect for a thread painting. He was kind enough to let me use it for this book, and here is the resulting thread painting. Beautiful artwork can be found in many places — books, Web sites, even packaging. Look at your friends' artwork or even your children's crayon drawings to find inspiration.

Materials

Note: Materials will vary depending on the quilt pattern choice.

One sheet inkjet-printable fabric, 8½" x 11"

Border fabrics, 45" wide

Flange fabric, 45" wide

Backing fabric, 45" wide

Lightweight batting

Tools and Notions

Thread

Darning foot

Sewing, embroidery and monofilament threads

Construction

Note: These general instructions work for any quilt pattern you want to use with your thread-painted artwork.

1. Print the artwork onto inkjet-printable fabric. Peel off the paper backing.

2. Layer the printed fabric over batting and pin the edges outside the design area.

3. Select threads that match the color of the artwork.

4. Set the machine for free-motion stitching; lower the feed dogs and install the darning foot.

5. Thread paint the design. As you "paint," be careful not to overwork it. If you add too much thread, the sketchy quality of the artwork can be lost. Less thread can be more effective, and you can always add more if needed.

6. Choose border fabrics that highlight the colors in your work. Remember that the borders are an extension of the artwork and they should flow one into the other.

7. After the thread painting is complete, trim the batting at the fabric block edge. Finish the quilt to complement your artwork

8. Quilt as you would any other wall hanging.

Denim Vest or Jacket — Two Ways

Size: Custom
Technique: Thread painting
Special focus: Thread painting as embroidery and from one printed design sheet
Skill level: Comfortable

I love art clothing, it allows me to express myself and to look different than everyone else. Often I make the garment and embellish it, but sometimes I find it easier to start with something I buy to customize. I have long loved denim jackets and vests for this reason. Many of them have a plain rectangular panel in the back that just begs to be decorated. This project allows you to start with a denim vest or jacket and make an amazing one of a kind garment with either a fabric as your thread painting base, or a design of your own.

Materials

Denim vest or jacket with a rectangular panel in the back

Complementary fabrics

Fabric for thread painted appliqué OR design printed onto computer printable fabric

Tools and Notions

Tracing paper

Paper-backed fusible web

Denim needles for machine

Thread

Beads, beaded trim, buttons, or other embellishments.

Making an appliquéd embroidery from fabric

1. Make a tracing paper mock-up of the size and shape of the back panel of the jacket or vest to be decorated.

2. Place the tracing paper template over the chosen fabric and decide what elements you will use and where they will be placed. Remember that you can take elements from anywhere in the fabric and move them to fit your design, as the elements will be cut out. (You can even take elements from different fabrics, as long as the scale of the designs relate to each other.) Trace them roughly onto the template so that you have a working guide.

3. Rough-cut around the elements you are using, and place them right-side up onto a paper-backed fusible product. Keep the paper on the underside of the fusible so that you are only fusing to the back of your fabric.

4. With the fusible attached to the back and the paper still in place, carefully cut around the edges of the design elements you are using.

5. Position these pieces onto the back of your garment and arrange so that you like the way they look. You can overlay your tracing paper template for the exact position, or simply move them around until you are happy with the composition.

6. Peel the paper off the back of the fusible and press the fabric into place. Read the instructions for your particular product, but it usually only takes a few seconds.

7. Thread paint your design using a denim needle. Make sure to bring your stitches over any cut edges so they will not ravel.

8. Embellish!

Creating a design on computer printable fabric

1. Make a tracing paper mock-up of the size and shape of the back panel of the jacket or vest to be decorated.

2. Print the design onto printable fabric. (I started with a photograph of a rug in my house and re-colored it in Photoshop.)

3. Complete the thread painting.

4. Decide on the placement for the thread painting on the back panel of the jacket or vest. Most likely, the panel will not be the same size as the printed design, and these areas will have to be filled in with strips of coordinating fabrics.

5. Sew strips of fabric to the top, bottom and sides of the thread painting so that it is slightly larger than the tracing paper template.

6. Position on the back of the garment and pin in place.

7. Turn the raw edges under so that there is a clean edge all around the thread painting. A zipper foot can get in close to the seam edges for a cleaner edge. Stitch into place with invisible thread (or use a decorative thread and even a decorative stitch, if you prefer).

8. Place some stitching through the thread painting to hold it to the garment.

9. Embellish.

Fabric Postcards

Finished size: May vary; Postcards shown are 3" x 5" up to 5" x 7"
Technique: Thread painting (Shown here, but sketches work too.)
Special focus: Quick and simple way for self expression
Skill level: Starter (and up)

Fabric postcards are all the rage these days. Give them as gifts, trade them, frame them, make them into quilts — these little art quilts are big on opportunities. Fancy threads, beads and other embellishments are part of the fun. Start with a photo, a fabric, or an original design. Many people use a traditional quilt binding, I find a satin or zigzag stitch around the edge does the trick and adds a punch of color.

Materials

Design; one of three ways

• Photo printed onto fabric

• Original design printed onto fabric

• Fabric with appropriately sized motif

Most fabric postcards are either 3" x 5" or 4" x 6", but there are no rules.

Thread

Batting

Backing fabric

Construction

1. Layer your design onto batting. (Fusible batting works well and then there is no need to pin.)

2. Begin thread painting. If only thread painting a small area, the batting is enough of a stabilizer; a lot of thread work may require a paper-backed stabilizer.

3. Pin on the backing fabric and trim all three layers to the size and shape desired.

4. Use a satin stitch or a zigzag with a short stitch length to create an edge. A small amount of quilting will add dimension and hold everything together.

5. Add beads and other embellishments.

Contributors and Resources

Many of the tools and supplies shown in this book are from the following manufacturers. Those marked with an asterisk generously contributed products for the samples in the book. Look for them at your local quilt, fabric or craft store; on the Internet or from a mail-order source.

For preprinted and custom kits and related supplies, order direct from author Leni Wiener.
www.LeniWiener.com

American and Efird, Inc. (A&E and Robison-Anton threads)
www.amefird.com

Atlas Gloves (Quilters' Gloves)
www.lfsinc.com

C. Jenkins (Bubble Jet Set 2000 and Bubble Jet Set Rinse)*
www.cjenkinscompany.com

Carol Doak (Foundation papers)*
www.caroldoak.com

Clover Needlecraft, Inc. (Sewing, cutting and quilting notions, and tools)
www.clover-usa.com

Coats & Clark (Dual Duty Plus thread)*
www.coatsandclark.com

Color Textiles (ColorPlus Printable Fabrics)*
www.colortextiles.com

Electric Quilt Company (Inkjet printable fabrics)*
www.electricquilt.com

Expo International (Trims)*
www.expointl.com

EZ Quilting by Wrights (Cutting and quilting tools, and notions)
www.ezquilt.com

Fairfield Processing Corp. (Batting and stuffing)
www.poly-fil.com

Fiskars Brands, Inc. (Cutting tools and supplies)
www.fiskars.com

Free Spirit Fabrics*
www.freespirit.com

Hobbs Bonded Fibers (Batting)
www.hobbsbondedfibers.com

June Tailor, Inc. (Sewing and quilting tools, and notions)
www.junetailor.com

Michael Miller Fabrics*
www.michaelmillerfabrics.com

Olfa (Rotary cutting tools, rulers and mats)
www.olfa.com

Pellon (Fleece and fusible web)*
www.shoppellon.com

WonderFil Threads (Threads)
www.wonderfil.net

Printed Treasures (Inkjet-printable fabrics)*
www.printedtreasures.com

Prym Consumer USA (Sewing, quilting and cutting tools and notions)
www.dritz.com

RJR Fabrics*
www.rjrfabrics.com

Rowenta (Irons and steamers)
www.rowenta.com

Roxanne Products Company (Hand appliqué and quilting tools)
www.thatperfectstitch.com

Schmetz (Sewing machine needles)*
www.schmetz.com

Sulky of America (Threads)
www.sulky.com

Superior Threads
www.superiorthreads.com

The Warm Company (Batting and fusible products)
www.warmcompany.com

Additional Resources

Tools and supplies shown in this book are also available from the following catalogs and Web sites:

Annie's Attic
1 Annie Lane
Big Sandy, TX 75755
(800) 582-6643
www.anniesattic.com

Clotilde LLC
P.O. Box 7500
Big Sandy, TX 75755-7500
(800) 772-2891
www.clotilde.com

Connecting Threads
P.O. Box 870760
Vancouver, WA 98687-7760
(800) 574-6454
www.ConnectingThreads.com

Ghee's
2620 Centenary Blvd. No. 2-250
Shreveport, LA 71104
(318) 226-1701
www.ghees.com

Herrschners, Inc.
2800 Hoover Road
Stevens Point, WI 54492-0001
(800) 441-0838
www.herrschners.com

Home Sew
P.O. Box 4099
Bethlehem, PA 18018-0099
(800) 344-4739
www.homesew.com

Keepsake Quilting
Route 25
P.O. Box 1618
Center Harbor, NH 03226-1618
(800) 865-9458
www.keepsakequilting.com

Nancy's Notions
333 Beichl Ave.
P.O. Box 683
Beaver Dam, WI 53916-0683
(800) 833-0690
www.nancysnotions.com

Sewing Machine Companies

Baby Lock
www.babylock.com

Husqvarna Viking Sewing Machine Co.
www.husqvarnaviking.com

Singer
www.singerco.com

Bernina of America
www.berninausa.com

Janome
www.janome.com

Tacony Corp.
www.tacony.com

Brother
www.brother-usa.com

Kenmore
www.sears.com

White
www.whitesewing.com

Elna USA
www.elnausa.com

Pfaff
www.pfaffusa.com

About the Author

Leni Levenson Wiener is a fiber artist and quilt instructor living in New Rochelle, New York. She holds a B.A. in Art History from Simmons College in Boston and a combined MA in Art Restoration/Conservation and Museology from the Universita Internazionale dell'Arte in Florence, Italy.

For many years Leni worked in the garment industry in New York City, designing private label lines for many department stores. She has also worked professionally as a commercial photographer.

In recent years, Leni has enjoyed working exclusively on her fiber art, teaching and lecturing on a variety of quilt techniques and quilt history. Thread Painting was a natural outgrowth of the things she loves — photography, sewing and art quilts.

Her own work is in contemporary art quilts and art clothing; her pieces are in many private collections and in several traveling shows. She prefers to work in a style that combines fabric collage and thread painting.

Please visit her Web site at www.LeniWiener.com for ready-made and custom thread painting kits, supplies and other resources.

Patterns

baby ball

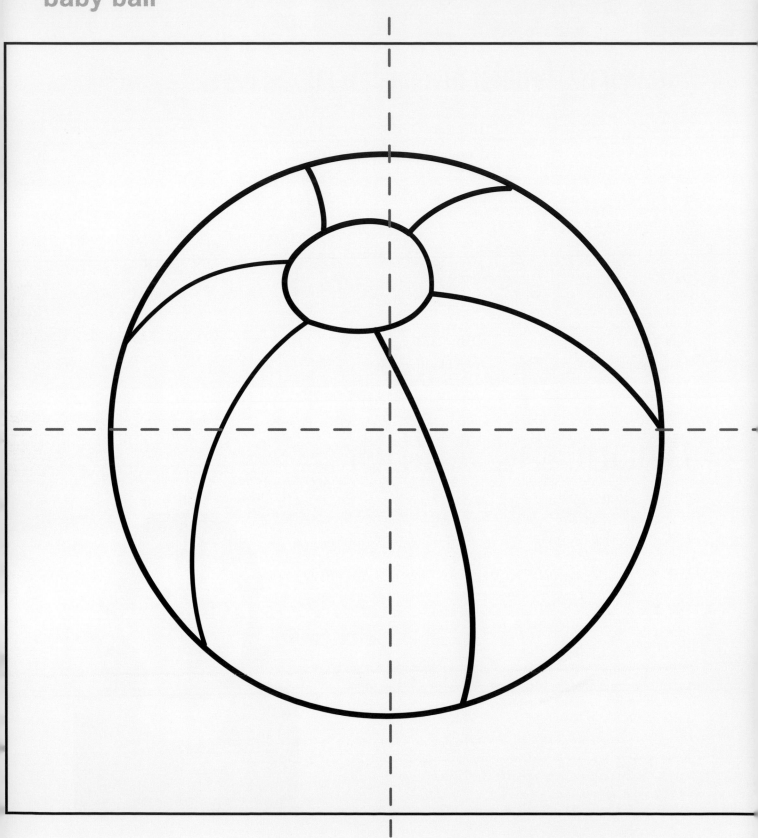

baby shoe

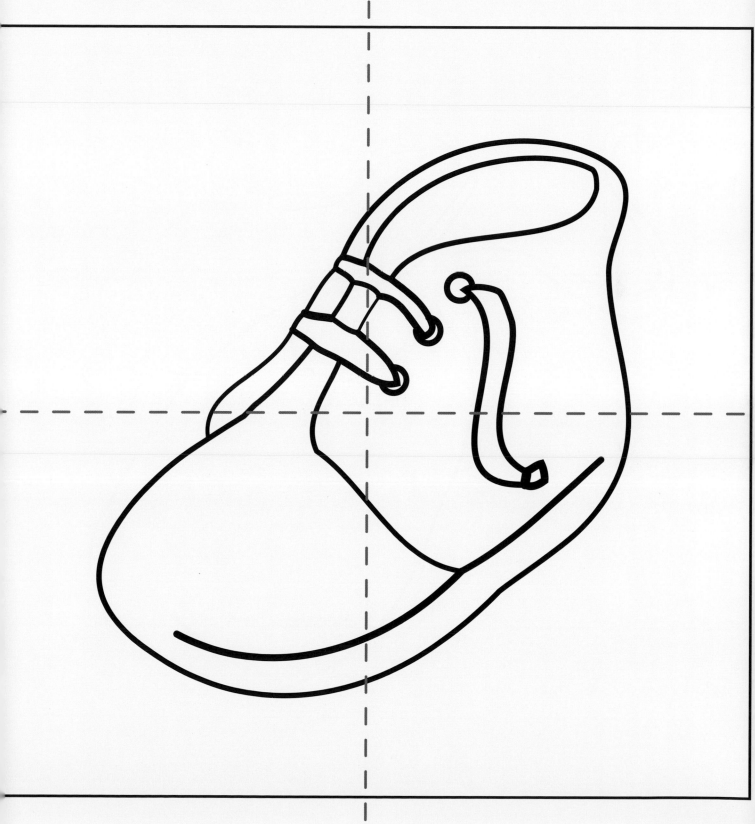

baby bib

baby duck

baby bib pattern

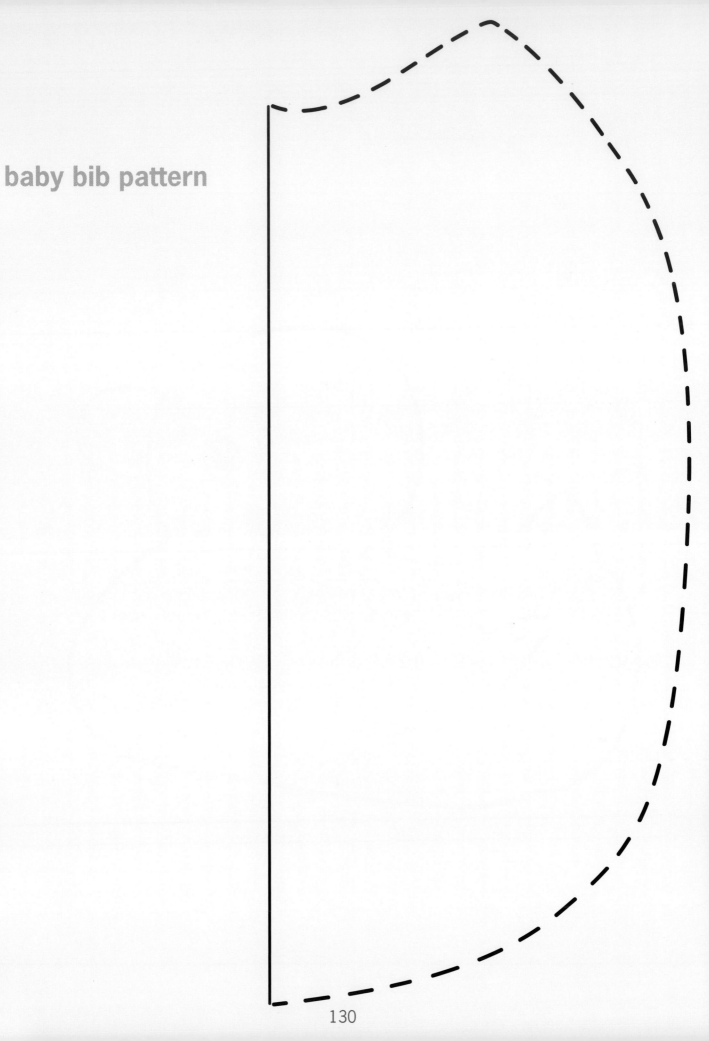

baby teddy bib

butterflies (enlarge 200%)

baby teddy quilt

joy

喜

dragonfly

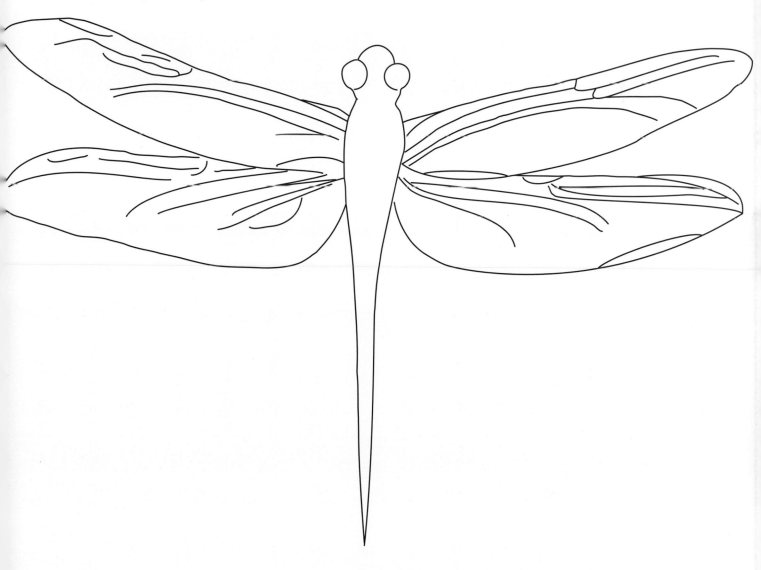

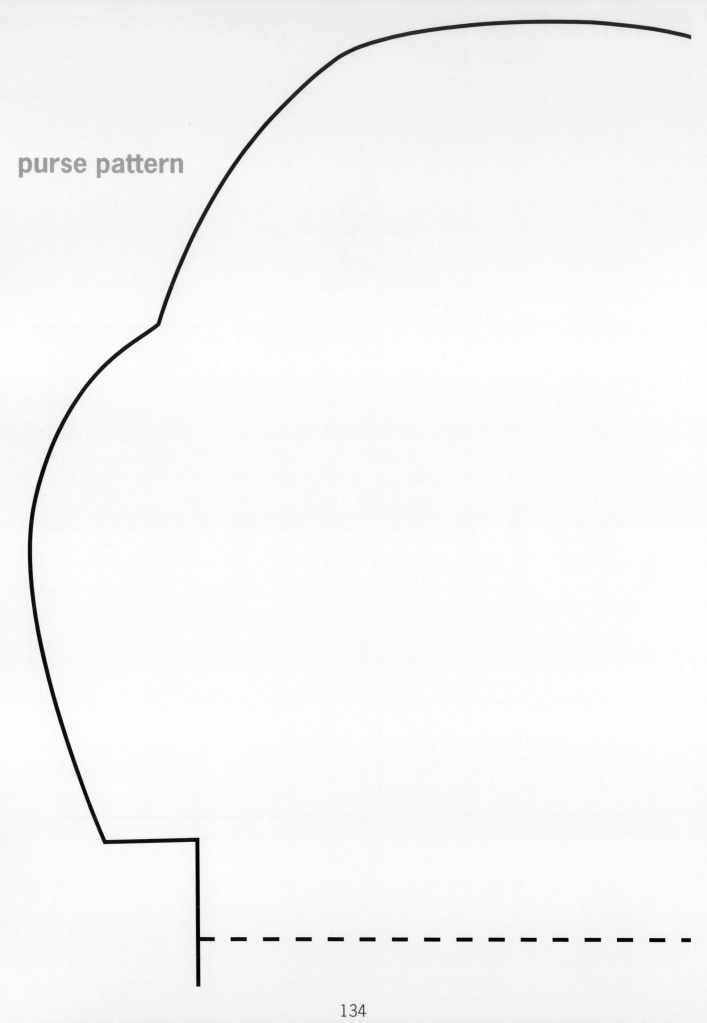

purse pattern

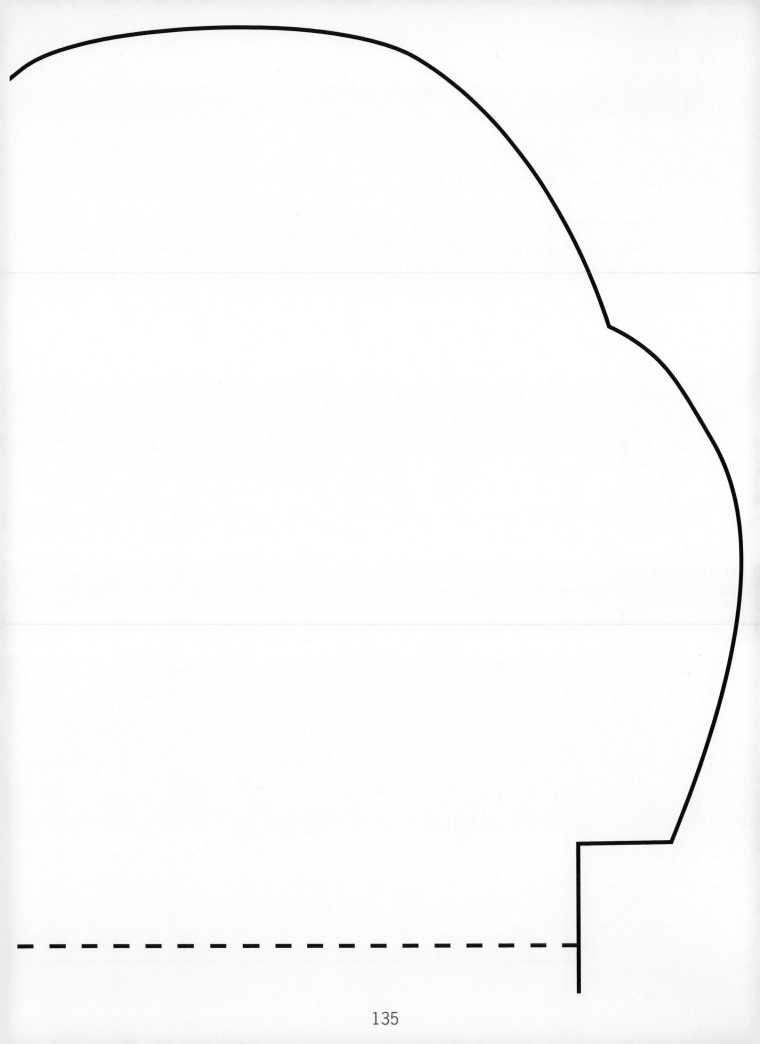

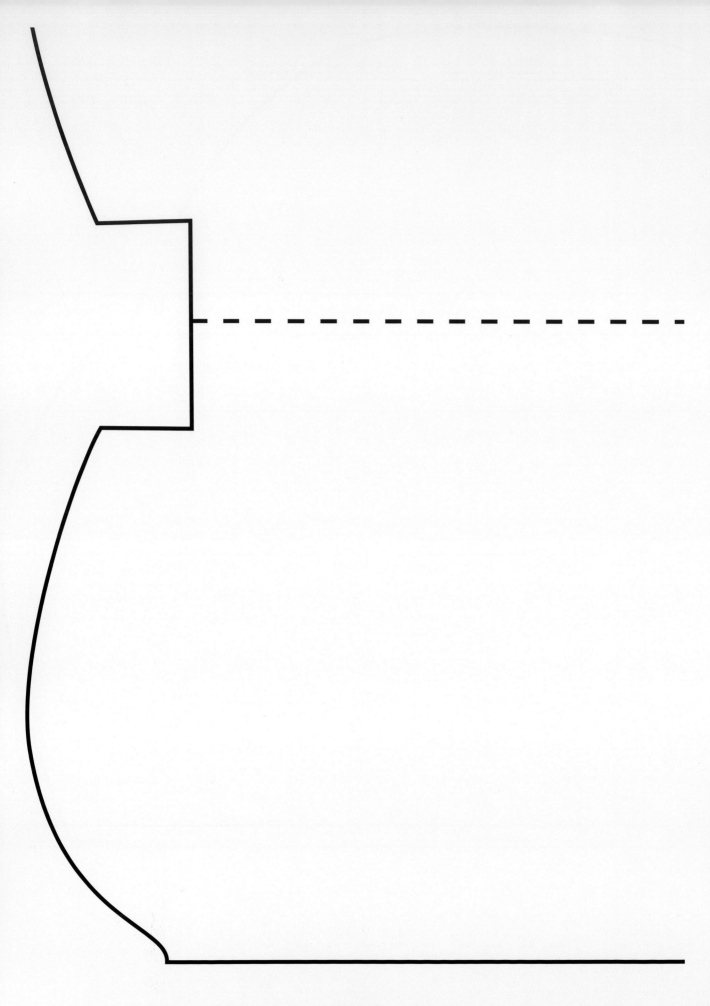

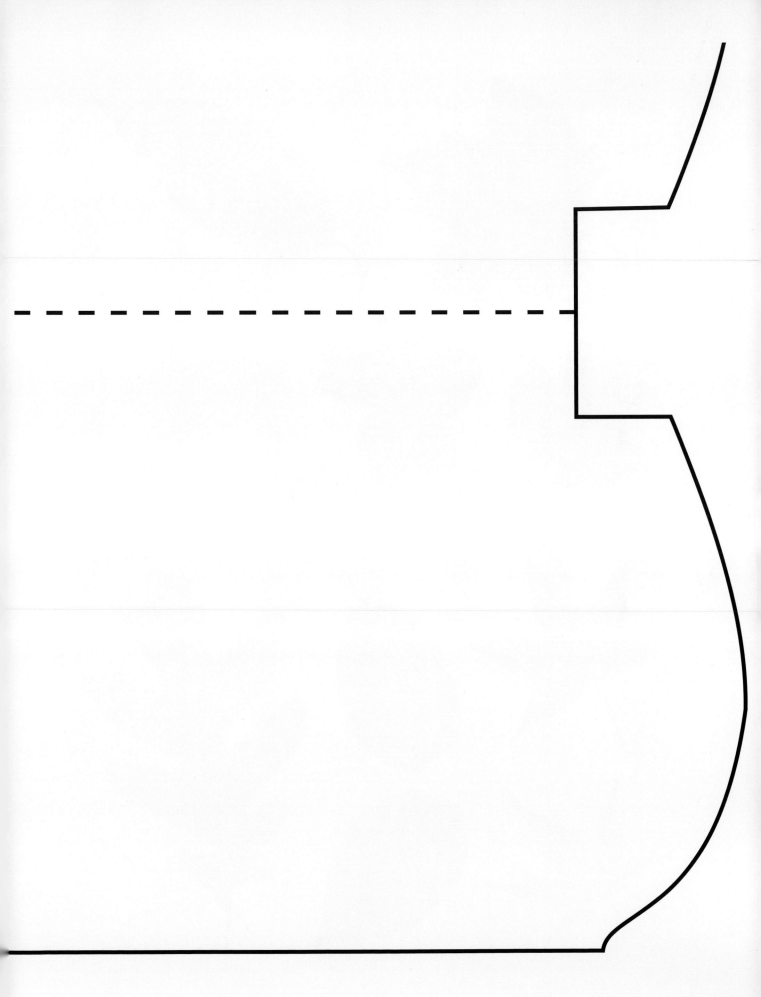

shirt designs

sitting girl left

sitting boy left

sitting girl right

sitting boy right

standing boy right

standing girl right

standing boy left

standing girl left

tea cup right

tea flowers

tea cup left

teapot

kuba cloth

Bring More Colorful Creativity to Your Sewing

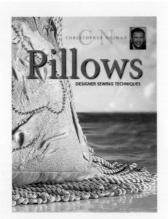

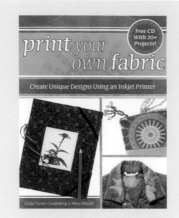

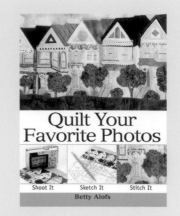